CONTENTS

Preface v

1. Emergen\ce of the Concepts of Business and Trade 1

2. 7 Ancipreneurship Lessons from the Greco-Roman Era 12

3. Stoicism in Ancient Rome: Four Takeaways for Budding Ancipreneurs 47

4. Ancient Shastras to Business Sutras: Six Lessons for Ancipreneurs 67

5. Ancipreneur Lessons from Hebraism, Christianity, and Islam 86

6. Tales From the Mediterranean Depths to the Pyramidal Peaks 94

7. The Learned Latin-Americans of Yore 111

8. Ancient Chinese Wisdom for Entrepreneurs 117

9. Inspiring Lessons from The Greatest Leaders in History 132

Contents

10. Business Lessons From Historical Events 153
11. Conclusion 168

References *173*
Web References *181*
Endnotes *187*
Acknowledgements *193*

ANCIPRENEUR:
ANCIENT PATHS FOR MODERN SUCCESS

UNLOCKING TIMELESS SECRETS FOR PROSPERITY, FULFILLMENT, AND WEALTH IN THE 21ST CENTURY

DR VIKAS KUMAR SINGH

Chennai • Bangalore

CLEVER FOX PUBLISHING
Chennai, India

Published by CLEVER FOX PUBLISHING 2024
Copyright © DR VIKAS KUMAR SINGH 2024

All Rights Reserved.
Paperback ISBN: 978-93-56489-20-2
Hardback ISBN: 978-93-56486-10-2

This book has been published with all reasonable efforts taken to make the material error-free after the consent of the author. No part of this book shall be used, reproduced in any manner whatsoever without written permission from the author, except in the case of brief quotations embodied in critical articles and reviews.

The Author of this book is solely responsible and liable for its content including but not limited to the views, representations, descriptions, statements, information, opinions and references ["Content"]. The Content of this book shall not constitute or be construed or deemed to reflect the opinion or expression of the Publisher or Editor. Neither the Publisher nor Editor endorse or approve the Content of this book or guarantee the reliability, accuracy or completeness of the Content published herein and do not make any representations or warranties of any kind, express or implied, including but not limited to the implied warranties of merchantability, fitness for a particular purpose. The Publisher and Editor shall not be liable whatsoever for any errors, omissions, whether such errors or omissions result from negligence, accident, or any other cause or claims for loss or damages of any kind, including without limitation, indirect or consequential loss or damage arising out of use, inability to use, or about the reliability, accuracy or sufficiency of the information contained in this book.

PREFACE

*I*n a world defined by relentless change and uncertainty, the foundations of business, entrepreneurship, and everyday life are shaking. Traditional strategies, those heralded as cutting-edge just a few years ago, have found themselves in the relentless grip of obsolescence. The turbulence of our era compels us to seek wisdom, not only in the latest trends but also in the timeless teachings of antiquity. The reality is that we are living in a highly competitive business environment which is totally unpredictable. This competitive environment of the 21st century has created a challenging landscape for businesses that includes drastic change at a very fast pace, a global borderless world, and a high dependence on technology. Due to this unpredictable business climate, companies struggle to forecast the future. Thus, they need to be able to quickly develop strategies that they can use whenever necessary in order to be more flexible. In order to accomplish this, they must acquire resources and develop the abilities that make it possible for them to act accordingly, depending on a changing scenario, or take the initiative in that situation.

So, my question is: how much can we rely just on technology and modern concepts? Or is there another dimension to look at the current challenges? Can we look towards ancient literature and seek solace from its wisdom? It could be learnings from the life of ancient philosophers, kings, or even texts and scriptures like The Bhagavad Gita, the epic verses of the Ramayana, or the profound wisdom contained in the Vedas. As I pen down the final words to this book, we have even a new Ram temple that has idols of Lord Ram at Ayodhya. With millions of people coming to this place, one thing is sure: despite all modernity, people have a belief in ancient scriptures. So, in this book, I not only look at Indian scriptures but wisdom from foreign countries as well: their texts, different religions, and published material. The ancient wisdom penned thousands of years ago has etched its way into the annals of human philosophy and spirituality. And yet, their guidance is not confined to temples, churches, mosques, shrines, or ashrams. Their relevance extends far beyond the spiritual realm, offering profound insights into the art of modern business and entrepreneurship. In these old journeys in time, we unearth ageless wisdom, which speaks to the very essence of our being. For example, The Bhagavad Gita imparts lessons of dharma (duty) and karma (action), instructing us to act with unwavering commitment to our purpose and without attachment to the outcomes. The Ramayana narrates the hero's journey of Lord Rama, a narrative of resilience, valour, and moral integrity, replete with lessons on leadership and ethical decision-making. The Vedas guide us to harmonise our actions with the natural order, creating sustainable and fulfilling livelihoods.

Yet, the ancient wisdom doesn't stop with the Vedic traditions of India. Across continents, cultures, and civilisations, there exists a wealth of knowledge that transcends time. From the Stoic philosophers who explored inner resilience in the face of adversity to the profound teachings of Chinese philosophers like Laozi and Confucius, who emphasised balance and ethical conduct, these teachings continue to resonate in our hearts.

Roman wisdom, with its emphasis on civic duty and the importance of governance, has lessons that extend into the boardrooms and offices of today. Hebrew texts illuminate the power of community and shared values. Islam and Christianity, with their moral codes and tales of endurance, offer guidance on ethics and purpose.

And let us not forget the general ideas of ancient times, as they are often the most accessible and universal. The simple yet profound tenets that form the bedrock of human civilisation—integrity, kindness, humility, and the pursuit of knowledge—speak to our shared humanity.

In a world driven by the pursuit of profits, shareholder value, and fleeting trends, we must ask ourselves: have we overlooked the enduring wisdom of our ancestors? Have we dismissed their teachings as irrelevant in the modern context? These days, budding entrepreneurs show a lot of promise as well as enthusiasm while undertaking any venture, but they often end up closing down their businesses. Despite using the best technological resources and a data-driven information base, they end up losing the whole business or closing down due to losses. Well, sometimes, things are beyond our control. However, many times, it's not the problem that is a challenge, but how we handle it or respond to that dictates the result of success or failure. It is precisely in these turbulent times, when we face challenges that our predecessors could not have imagined that we must turn to the ancient wisdom that has weathered the test of time.

In the chapters that follow, we will explore how the sacred verses and timeless philosophies from across the world can illuminate the path forward. We will witness how these ancient insights can be woven into the fabric of contemporary business, entrepreneurship, and everyday life. Our journey will take us through the corridors of history and the annals of wisdom, revealing that amidst the chaos of the present, the answers we seek may lie hidden in the echoes of the past.

Ancipreneur – A Concept Towards New Paradigm

As entrepreneurs, we are loaded today with information, artificial intelligence, technology, and software that can immensely help us in our day-to-day business activities. But the real question is: what is the foundation of this business? What are the ethical and moral parameters of this business? Why do we conduct a particular business? How can history and philosophical concepts help us in our modern business?

I strongly believe that if we, entrepreneurs, possess historical knowledge, it definitely unlocks the door to a world of opportunities, enticing us to unravel our true potential and leave all unsolved mysteries to abeyance. We can discover a newer soul if we truly learn the ancient wisdom from the history of the world. This process involves searching for the true meaning of your goals and purpose. History in business is more than just a mundane exercise for scholars; it's an invaluable tool that reveals the unexplored secrets to success. Just like a painter brings life to a blank canvas, interpreting an ancient quote or exploring ancient text can unlock a treasure trove of knowledge. It's akin to deciphering intricate financial data, where every number holds its own significance and must be interpreted with precision. Trust me, it's no walk in the park! It's not easy!

If we look back a few decades, Joseph Alois Schumpeter (1883-1950) said that an entrepreneur is the cornerstone of capitalism—the source of innovation. But if you see in reality, the concept of entrepreneurship has been badly misunderstood. It is said that Richard Cantillon, an Irish economist, made popular the term "entrepreneur" in the 18th century. According to him, an entrepreneur is a person who buys factory services at a certain price with a view to selling his product at another price. However, the credit for coining the term "entrepreneur" also goes to French economist Jean Baptiste Say, who gave expression to this word in about 1800. The word originates from the French word "Entreprendre," which means to "undertake." So, it infers that an entrepreneur is a person who makes money by starting or running businesses, and it involves financial risks. Therefore, an entrepreneur is an individual having an exclusive idea to establish a new venture.

However, if we look at reality, we find that most of the entrepreneurs who start a business are not successful. They often fail, and this failure could be for multiple reasons. But my opinion is that the concept of "entrepreneur" itself has gone out of time, and we need to have some new definition that can help entrepreneurs to be more successful in their ventures. The need of the hour is that we redefine this whole concept and view it from different perspectives. In my opinion, there could be various ways to do so. However, I prefer to look towards the past and help our modern entrepreneurs get some wisdom from ancient times. This knowledge can help them to transform themselves into '**Ancipreneurs**.' I first used the term "Ancipreneur" in my TEDx talk in February 2023. I firmly believe that the world now needs "Ancipreneurs." We need to ensure that all entrepreneurs now equip themselves with ancient wisdom. They need to implement in their businesses a knowledge that can effortlessly use ancient wisdom and harmoniously apply it to the present scenario. Exploring historical events can offer a captivating perspective on markets and marketing strategies, exposing intricate connections with the larger business world. The conundrums of marketing may not be novel or singular, but they still pack a punch! By peeling back layers of history, we unearth long-lost marketing gems and innovations that have been buried in the sands of time. And by studying these forgotten details, we can avoid making the same mistakes twice and forge a brighter marketing future.

Summarised within this table are insights obtained from written works authored by ancient philosophers all over the world touching on the wisdom that was prevalent in those periods. I feel the concept of 'ancipreneurship' gels well when it comes to exploring past published information and trying to see how entrepreneurs and an era of entrepreneurship can be revived again with some new perspective that has a touch of ancient times.

Table 1: Evidence from literature for creating and transforming entrepreneurs

Ancient Text/s	Scholar/ Philosopher	Entrepreneurial Lessons
On Rhetoric *The Nichomachean Ethics* *The Politics*	Aristotle	Reputation management Business communication Leadership Sustainability Morality in business Opportunity-driven course of action
The Republic *The Apology*	Plato	Leadership Realistic expectations Open-mindedness Socratic philosophy Critical thinking Innovation
Oeconomicus. *Memorabilia*	Xenophon	Obstacles to opportunity Risk-taking
Orations and Speeches	Demosthenes Isocrates	Virtue and best practices Wealth management
Arthashashtra *Upanishads* *Ramayana,* *Mahabharata*	Kautilya Various Rishis Rishi Valmiki, Vyas	Character building Business ethics Self-restraint Purity of thought Action

The Analects	Confucius	Righteousness
		Resilience
		Restraint
Torah, Kaballah	Moses (*Sources also name other Rabbis as contributors*)	Will-power
		Overcoming fear
		Power of negotiations

Based on these teachings, we find that there are valuable lessons for entrepreneurs and people who are already running their businesses or want to enter the business. In fact, institutions devoted to the understanding of entrepreneurship and its various facets are increasingly persuading students to analyse the evolution of this 'art' through the lens of history. For instance, the Ewing Marion Kauffman Foundation is educating the public on the economic models and theories adopted by successful entrepreneurs all over the world and across timelines. As we march ahead onto further chapters in this book, we will learn from the decisions of our ancestors, from the conquests and failures of mighty rulers, from the springs of explorations to the overflowing wells of revolutionary ideas and many other ancient teachings that we have forgotten by us in our quest to learn from concepts of the modern era.

CHAPTER 1

EMERGENCE OF THE CONCEPTS OF BUSINESS AND TRADE

*H*istorians have attributed the growth of early entrepreneurship and commercial enterprises to Middle Eastern merchant families from Assyrian to Babylonian times who were involved in exporting excess textiles and metals, as well as importing necessary goods. Even before the commencement of monetary transactions, early business transactions thrived on the seemingly archaic concept of 'trade and barter,' which was a convenient need-based system for societies to exchange goods and services.[i] There have been early pieces of evidence of Mesopotamian tribes around 6000 BC engaging in this form of trade, which was subsequently adopted by other cultures.

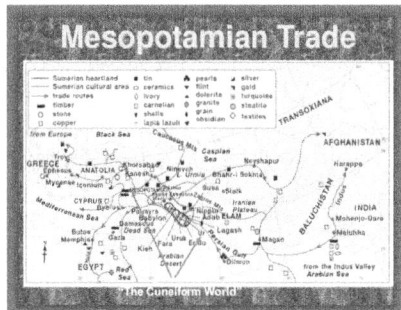

Source: google.co.uk (https://www.pinterest.com/pin/361976888796704395/)

Entrepreneurial evidences in Egypt, the Indus Valley, Greece and Rome are sparsely documented, and thereby, the development of enterprise has been thought to be late in its advent. Inscriptions and cuneiform scripts, mostly of Neo-Babylonian nature, provide the earliest form of documentation regarding the primitive forms of entrepreneurship. Debt management, the emergence of land markets, management of finances with record-keeping, and export and import of surplus and deficit, respectively, are clearly marked in the pages of history. Royal inscriptions and palace archives show that city temples and palaces acted as centres of storage, production and trade of bulk goods. These public institutions engaged with merchants, who possessed considerable capital of their own that they could invest in the trading of goods. These merchants were the early entrepreneurs and were referred to by many local titles like Sumerian damgar or the Babylonian tamkarum. The term "ENTREPRENEUR" came in the 17th century. Johannes Renger has pointed out that an entrepreneur "denoted" a person who entered into a contractual relationship with the government for the performance of a service or the supply of goods. The price at which the contract was valued was fixed, and the entrepreneurs bore the risks of profit and loss from the bargain.

At the speed of a click, the world is now united in trading goods and ideas through modern technology! Journey back in time to 2,000 years ago, and it becomes an insurmountable task for global trade to flourish. Thanks to the Silk Route, the first step towards world supply chains could be taken.

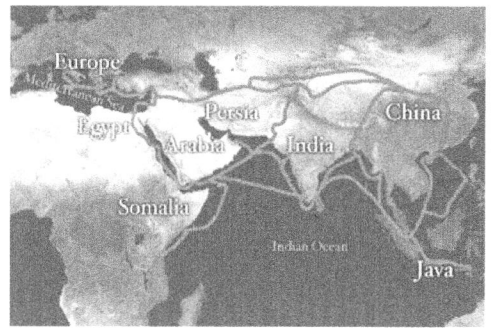

Source: https://nammu.com/eng/lapis-lazuli-trade-routes/

Threading together the world's major settlements, the incredible Silk Route stretched over 5,000 miles of land and sea - a web of vibrant trade and shared language that connected cultures from the 2nd century BCE. The original Silk Route—the dynastic highway to distant China, got its name from the beautiful Chinese silks. Zhang Quian, a renowned Chinese official and diplomat, launched this journey during the Han Dynasty, gaining even more momentum in the Tang dynasty. Trade along the luxurious Silk Road was highly valued, and merchants were supported with plenty of opportunities to profit! Advances in technology and greater political stability turbocharged trade along these routes! As the trade routes opened up, exotic animals, tantalising spices and novel ideas began to be exchanged day by day.

With hardy horses from the Ferghana Valley (also known as "heavenly horses" or "blood-sweating horses") and domesticated camels, the traders acted as the transporters as well as relationship managers between the producers and customers.[ii, iii] Culturally, it had a lot of significance as it connected cultures—Buddhism began to spread, Sanskrit texts were translated into different languages, and new religions emerged.

With marine trade flourishing after the second century BC, business in Italy and Greece also became prominent with an influx of merchants and vendors. Athenians received numerous forms of stimulus for entrepreneurship, such as manufacturing, mining, agriculture, and finance, with initiatives including legal policies for private and public funding, issuance of security collateral, along a sound educational system termed paideia that instilled free thought and ethical practices.[iv,v] If we compare another city-state in Greece like Sparta, it is evident that the reinforcement of enterprising behaviour accompanied by restoring justice gave Athens a better financial standing as opposed to Spartans, who relied heavily on state resources and neighbouring countries. In fact, Sparta was more focussed on military might and making its citizens ready to defend Sparta. Similarly, if we see Western Europe, Fritsch et al. (2021) indicate that Rome's domination over Southern Germany for two thousand years led to wealthier socio-economic ideology due to amplified cultural imprinting access than other regions.

Source: Getty Images (DEA / M. SEEMULLER / Contributor form DeAgostini Collection) Cited in https://www.historyextra.com/period/medieval/genghis-khan-mongol-warlord-conquered-world-china-medieval/

In the 15th century, the Mongol invasions sparked a new era of exploration as these joined Europe and Asia in a historic embrace, forging an eternal link of East-West relations. With peace and order quickly reigned after the Mongols conquered new lands, they opened their doors to friendly international relations with open arms. The Mongols never wavered from claiming universal power, yet they still welcomed foreigners - all the way to China! Merchants, artisans and envoys alike explored uncharted lands under their rule. Travelling along the ancient Silk Roads, traders brought exotic Asian goods to Europe, inspiring a great quest to find a sea route to Asia. Trade was an integral part of the nomadic Mongol lifestyle, and merchants were held in high esteem—a refreshing contrast to many other ancient societies.

Their spirit of cooperation is a textbook lesson on teamwork for entrepreneurs, as it is written in their records that "when it was wet, we bore the wet together; when it was cold, we bore the cold together."

The Mongols established the Ortogh, which were essentially merchant associations to ensure that those involved in long-distance trade benefitted from improved social statuses. Making life easier for merchants, they boosted the supply of paper money and slashed tariffs - a win-win situation! Experiencing a stunning upturn, trade flourished across and through Eurasia! Similar to the modern-day concept of limited liability, principals were responsible for losses that topped their initial investment, whereas ortoghs had none of this burden to bear. And of course, with the merchants there came physicians, scientists and artisans, travelling ceaselessly throughout the Mongol regions in Eurasia—giving rise to an unparalleled interflow of knowledge and culture resonating powerfully throughout the world, China included.

Between the 1600s and 1700s, the Ottoman Empire was a hub of economic brilliance and diversity! Strategically located at the crossroads of three bustling trading routes—Europe, Asia and

Africa—the empire enjoyed unprecedented wealth and success through compelling trade opportunities. Through clever melds of traditional and modern economic models, the Ottoman Empire crafted a dynamic and intricate economy. The Ottomans expanded their empire through war conflicts with the Byzantine Empire, Safavid Empire, the conquests of Bulgaria, Serbia and the famous acquisition of Constantinople. Silk Road trade networks had enriched the Ottomans for centuries. However, new sea routes that bypassed Ottoman trade routes shifted the power away.

The Ottoman conquest of Constantinople with the victory of Ottoman Sultan Mehmed II (Source: Public Domain Wikipedia Image)

How were these trade routes discovered? Let us probe further into the adventures of the explorers that were going on concurrently with the exciting invasions around the world.

In 1453, the Constantinople-based Crusader dream came to an abrupt end when the Ottoman Turks asserted their dominance and imposed a ban on Christian traders. While the Portuguese had a newfound way to trade around the tip of Africa, Spaniards were stopped in their tracks due to a treaty that blocked them from accessing it without a Portuguese license - talk about unexpected twists and turns! Christopher Columbus saw the challenge of conquering the Turks and Portuguese as a chance to rethink traditional trade routes and discover a new, more efficient way of exchanging goods that would stand the test of time. His claims that the earth wasn't flat but spherical were met with scepticism, but he didn't give up. Guiding a host of brave adventurers, he ventured into unexplored lands of uncertainty. Columbus' daring leadership made the impossible possible. On October 7, 1492, Columbus set sail to uncharted territory - only to be met by vast flocks of birds and instinctively change course till the crew spotted land on October 12th! Unearthing the mysterious trade winds, Columbus cleverly exploited the North Atlantic's cyclical winds to chart his two-way voyage across the oceans. Struggling against the relentless sea, he would have been deprived of much-needed sustenance without the assistance of the winds—but thankfully, he made it home.

One cannot forget the contribution of Vasco de Gama in the discovery of a trade route to India. In Europe, the exotic flavours of India captivated the taste buds. Just imagine how, in those days, the only way to travel from Europe to India was on foot! This journey was an investment of both time and money!

The King of Portugal sought fortune and glory by discovering a sea route to India - where spices waited to be explored! Tasked with uncovering a passage to India, King Manuel I of Portugal supplied the pioneering explorer Vasco da Gama with a fleet of ships and set him off on an epic adventure across Africa! On July 8, 1497, he embarked on a journey of a lifetime from the great city of Lisbon, Portugal. He led a veritable armada of 174 sailors and vessels. The daring crew of the expedition bravely navigated around the impenetrable Cape of Good Hope, conquering the southern tip of Africa! A skilled navigator was discovered in the heart of Africa! Harnessing the power of the monsoon winds and his own vast knowledge, they managed to traverse the Indian Ocean in a month or less, making it all the way to Calicut, India. Though the return journey wasn't as smooth, he undertook two more voyages towards the east, committing himself to lead generations of merchant seafarers through correct and safer routes.

With the growing demand for spices, across ancient times in India, bustling trade centres had emerged—Patliputra, Peshawar, Taxila, Indraprastha, Mithila, Maduram, Surat, Ujjain and Kanchi, to name a few—as hubs of import and export. If we jump into the world of India's ancient trade and explore its flourishing market, we will find it brimming with a vast array of items such as spices, wheat, sugar, indigo, opium, sesame oil, cotton and even parrots! This glorious culture had writers like Megasthenes and Fa-Hein to Xavierzang singing praises of this bustling 'Swaran Bhoomi' - touting it to be the richest economy in the world! However, under the oppressive rule of the East India Company, India lost its autonomy - robbed of their home-grown products, they were forced to export raw materials in exchange for expensive imported goods. During India's freedom struggle, the 'Swadeshi' movement for indigenous products became a war cry. After independence, India and its entrepreneurs have done a wonderful transformation, which all Indians should feel proud of.

Although Greece is supposed to be rich in culture, several Indian scriptures, including the Upanishads, Arthashashtra (Indian economic guidebook), and Bhagavad Gita, provide valuable ancient wisdom. If interpreted correctly, this knowledge can be easily applied by today's entrepreneurs.

So, let me add more on Eastern concepts. Truly speaking of Eastern Philosophy, even orientalism is deeply incorporated into modern entrepreneur lessons; Confucian values speak in favour of a 'sage mindset' that aids mental healthfulness and cognitive sharpness when addressing difficulties within the world of business start-ups. It further advises 'Ren Yi' wisdom contexts towards benevolence/holiness being necessary aspects of Qing (positive emotions) along with Li (correctness), both being paramount determinants in current-day SME Chinese entrepreneurs' entrepreneurial decisions, which was uncovered during a study.

Evidence from ancient Rome, China, the Renaissance period in Europe, Middle Ages pertaining to various models of entrepreneurship, as well as assessing how productive/unproductive various enterprises proved to be, were collected. Lessons from this initial evidence pave the way for our further discussion ahead.

Table 2: Classic theories of 'successful entrepreneurs' given by early economists on the basis of historical pieces of evidence adapted from the compilation by Praag et al.

Social scientist/ philosopher	Published Text/ Source	Concept of an entrepreneur
Richard Cantillon	'Essai sur la Nature du Commerce en Général' (1755)	-Add value to society's economic value -Arbitrager, risk-bearer
Jean-Baptiste Say	A Treatise on Political Economy or the Production, Distribution and Consumption of Wealth -1803, 1971!	Coordinator between production and distribution, modern leader and manager
Alfred Marshall	Principles of Economics (1890)	Suppliers of commodities, drivers of innovations, and progressive cost-minimizers should have specialisation in the area with resources at hand.

Joseph Schumpeter	The Theory of Economic Development (1911)	Innovator and leader – not a risk taker, manager or capitalist. Continuous flux of innovation driving towards change and creation.
Frank Knight	Risk, Uncertainty and Profit (1921)	Uncertainty bearer and overcoming through capital and foresight.
Kirzner	Competition and Entrepreneurship (1973)	Exploitation of profit opportunities, decision-making, owner of resources.

If we read them, we will find that these ancient concepts and traits of entrepreneurship still hold good today. The concept of 'ancipreneurship' that I talk about is basically focussed on the ancient wisdom with which we all would be able to navigate through archives with Sherlock-like precision, uncover cause and effect relationships akin to piecing together a puzzle, and present all relevant facts in a way that guarantees nothing gets left out. With this mindset of "ancipreneurship" on your side, you'll have all the tools to make you a successful business person. Even if you don't do any business, these concepts can be true life-changing wisdom that will help you even in your day-to-day living!

CHAPTER 2

7 ANCIPRENEURSHIP LESSONS FROM THE GRECO-ROMAN ERA

*T*he citizens of the ancient Greco-Roman era built a system of incentives into their values and institutions, prompting people to take part in entrepreneurial activities and use any wealth created for the benefit of society. Most companies (chiefly those in Athens) were small-scale, individual projects managed by the proprietor as a free citizen or freedman (or a metic, i.e. foreigner) with assistance from a few servants. For citizens and metics, achieving entrepreneurial success was an opportunity to advance socially and economically, while for slaves, it often meant gaining their freedom.

Image Source: sidiropoulos.medium.com

Athens was the first society to have substantial entrepreneurship and management. They created the right incentives to spark entrepreneurship. When managing enterprises, they emphasised the division of labour and building up knowledge and skills. Furthermore, different legal institutions were established to uphold law and order, as well as validate the incentives in place.[vi, vii, viii, ix]

The Pyramid of Influence: Aristotle's persuasion theory that can be applied by Ancipreneurs

In his renowned treatise, *Rhetoric*, Aristotle proposed a framework for persuasive communication, which has been referenced frequently by many business and management specialists over time. The ability to convince someone to change their actions or beliefs is called persuasion. Crafting a convincing argument requires making a reasonable demand, proving your credibility, and displaying the direct and indirect advantages of granting your request to the audience.

When constructing a message for an audience, logos (facts), pathos (emotional appeal), and ethos (moral standing) should all be taken into account. Logos consists of providing facts and evidence to back up your argument. Pathos is the method of leveraging your audience's emotions, like fear or enthusiasm. At last, presenting your expertise, character, and intentions to your audience can help earn their trust through ethos.[x, xi]

Understanding who your target audience is and what they are drawn to is an essential part of business. Knowing the needs and interests of your audience will allow you to craft a message that connects with them. Before attempting to influence your audience, it is important to build trust by introducing your credibility. Business owners of start-ups can use Aristotle's ideas on persuasion to effectively communicate their message to their potential investors and realise their objectives.[xii, xiii, xiv, xv]

Knowing the key principles of persuasion will help businesses develop powerful and effective marketing campaigns. For instance, logos are utilised by businesses to showcase facts and evidence about their product or service. Logos entails providing proof of logic to bolster an argument. Consequently, we should make sure that any details or facts that we share are accurate and trustworthy.

Pathos tries to emotionally connect with an audience by referencing shared values and beliefs. To achieve this, we should always invest time in understanding the needs and interests of the audience so that we can craft our message based on it. Lastly, you can build ethos by showing that you are credible and trustworthy through exhibiting knowledge and high moral values. To achieve this, we can make sure that my messages come off as professional and friendly at the same time to avoid turning away my readers. These elements of persuasion are essential for effective communication in business settings.

The *ethos* method of persuasion involves creating trust and credibility by demonstrating good character and ethical principles. It involves creating authoritative and trustworthy impressions through ethical behaviour and demeanour. This form of persuasion capitalises on the fact that people are more likely to listen to and be persuaded by somebody who is highly respected and trustworthy. In business, the ethos mode of persuasion can be used to build relationships with customers.

According to Robert Plutchik's research in 2001, there are eight main emotions: joy, trust, fear, surprise, sadness, anticipation, anger, and disgust. According to Plutchik, emotions are more than just feeling. Emotion involves many interrelated stages, starting with exposure to a stimulus and encompassing feelings, psychological alterations, impulses to act, and purposeful behaviour. In other words, feelings don't form in a vacuum. Emotions are reactions to significant experiences in an individual's life and often drive people to take action. Through the use of pathos, the speaker or writer creates an emotional bond with the audience.

Andrew Dlugan says, "*It is vital for speakers to strive to create a shared feeling between themselves and their listeners.*" Pathos involves the capability to produce emotions in the audience and connect these reactions with parts of your speech in a calculated manner.

Brand Stories that readers can relate to above-mentioned concepts

As entrepreneurs, we are always trying to develop products or communicate our message so that our target group can relate to it. So, any company or brand has to pass the test of ethics, logos and Pathos. So, let me highlight a few brands that have highly impressed me with the above concepts.

Apple – This brand strives to help every person reach their fullest potential through technology. When expressing this idea, they use language that is straightforward, genuine, and easy to understand.

A quick glance at Apple's website reveals that, unlike other consumer technology companies who use technical jargon, Apple keeps their brand message plain, accessible, and benefit-focused. There are always people talking about Apple's latest designs or comments from the founder, latest events and ventures. A constant buzz is important for the brand, and this buzz has to be not just about the products but also about the people working on them. That's called building a real connection!

Victoria's Secret - In 2014, the American lingerie company Victoria's Secret received a lot of criticism over a campaign with the slogan "The Perfect 'Body,'" which appeared on images of their "Body" lingerie line featuring ultrathin supermodels. This suggested that being thin and flawless was the ideal image for a "perfect body." The majority of women cannot attain these bodies safely. Many saw this as detrimental to women's mental health and self-esteem, with a risk of promoting unhealthy dieting habits and eating disorders. People were outraged and created an online backlash, leading to a petition of over 30,000 signatures demanding the company apologise and take corrective measures for the insensitive ad. Hence, Victoria's Secret modified the slogan to "A Body for Every Body."

Old Spice - The TV commercial titled "The Man Your Man Could Smell Like" from Old Spice was a perfect combination of pathos and logos. Humour and drama can be effective ways to showcase the qualities of your products and have a lasting impression on the viewers. When done well, theatrics, acting, and scripts in your advertisement can produce incredible results. This ad was successful and won many awards. It has also been imitated and mocked in many movies and TV shows.

Colgate - Colgate has a strong history of creating effective advertising campaigns and implementing successful marketing strategies. Colgate has effectively resonated with and engaged the public through its emotionally compelling narratives. In January 2020, a campaign called "Smile Karo Aur Shuru Ho Jao" was launched, featuring real-life stories aimed at promoting hope and courage.

It is noteworthy to mention how Colgate appealed to local customers through the power of persuasion. Colgate's marketing tactics hit the bullseye in their strategy centred on the Kumbh Mela—the grandest congregation of Hindu worshipers. They set up booths wherein all the pilgrims would be bestowed with free samples of Colgate toothpaste and an opportunity to win thrilling prizes!

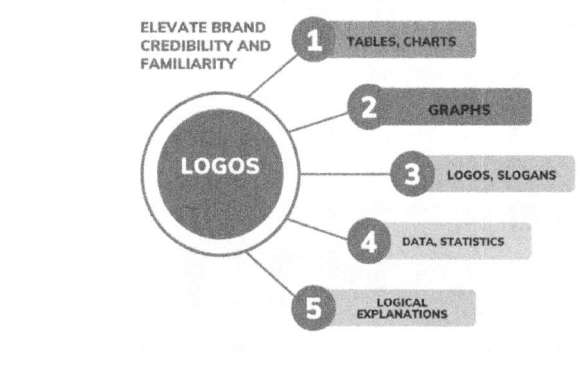

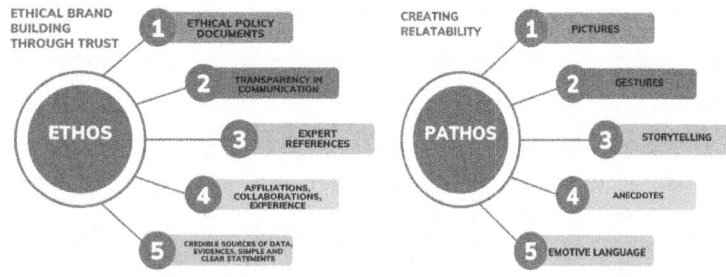

Transforming thinking and conversations: Socrates as a social entrepreneur

Socrates, a masterful communicator, was known as the 'wisest man on the earth" during his times. He would always ask questions and seek answers from people. He would not take any fact or statement at face value but would always go deeper. Socrates advised people of his time to have *conversations*. He believed in questions and answers so that we could debate upon a subject and go to its roots to understand it. But as readers, do you find some semblance with our Bhagwat Gita? As we all know, the Gita is also in the question-and-answer format. Krishna keeps answering questions of Arjun and the more they discuss, the more clarity is achieved during the "conversation." It is the same thing we find in the Socrates's way of seeking the truth.

Socrates was passionate about teaching the younger generation his famous phrase, "Know thyself." So, my dear readers, as entrepreneurs, the first task is to honestly assess yourself! Developing self-awareness as well as knowledge of yourself, your business, and the industry you're entering is essential for a successful start. Realise your full potential by conducting an honest SWOT analysis. So, let me emphasise knowing yourselves, and this is what Socrates, the ancient Greek philosopher, used to remind himself. The Latin version of this phrase is "nosce te ipsum." It's incredibly important for entrepreneurs to understand and be aware of themselves as it helps them understand their capabilities and purpose.

One of his popular quotes says, "Everyone wants to tell you what to do and what's good for you. They don't want you to find your own answers; they want you to believe theirs." It is an important indicator for all entrepreneurs to stand by their decisions if they know in their hearts that they are right. Socrates squashed gossip swiftly. When encountered by a young man telling a story about Jona, Socrates asked him three questions—whether he knew what he was going to say about Jona to be completely true, whether it would adversely affect Jona and when the young man confusedly nodded, he proceeded to ask if he still wanted to share the information. He always believed that *"strong minds discuss ideas, average minds discuss events, weak minds discuss people."*

The Socratic method is a questioning technique that starts by asking an individual a question and then developing the conversation further based on their answer. The process involves an iterative approach to establish an idea that is more specific based on a general concept. We want to assist someone in their reasoning and provide them with a solution. Through questioning, the person seeks out logical reasons and potential ways to enhance the situation. It is designed to discourage a person from blindly accepting facts and ideas, encouraging them instead to think for themselves. It elevates analysis as it unveils things that the decision-maker may not have considered while analysing.

Now, as an entrepreneur or a business person or a CEO of any company, all can gain benefit from the Socratic Method as they usually have a few assumptions regarding the best solution to choose. In general, the product/service of a business solves a problem. It can be further refined if we figure out what these assumptions are actually based on. When having dialogue in terms of the Socratic Method, it cannot only focus on passing information or sharing ideas. Negative comments made by customers, personnel, or competitors have to be taken into account. This inspires companies to plan for difficult situations ahead of time. The collective intel of a group helps entrepreneurs and businesses craft successful strategies within their reach and come up with creative alternatives as well. Regularly gauging company beliefs gives clearness about its mission; this sharpens everyone's focus so that there is an agreed-upon target and responsibility consequently assumed by all members.

Disruption often comes from challenging traditional assumptions, creating new possibilities. We can broaden our perspectives by surrounding ourselves with people who possess different sets of ideas and doctrines. At the heart of the Socratic method is openness to new concepts and the creation of close relationships through which knowledge can be exchanged. A variety of opinions makes decision-making better, as it encourages challenging assumptions.[xvi, xvii, xviii] Usually, most business owners and managers typically work in environments that don't encourage or accept creativity, and the people they deal with e have varied levels of creative ability. According to Sonnenberg and Goldberg (2007), the Socratic Method is an effective way of building a learning-conducive environment and encouraging creativity in an unpredictable setting. Philip Dennett's (2014) paper outlined and subjected to empirical testing a model that firms can use to promote creativity within the company through a questionnaire-discussion-feedback cycle.ˣⁱˣ

Source: *Library of Congress/science Photo Library.*

Let's take up the example of Ford Motor Company to describe how the Socratic principles have been successfully applied. Henry Ford had a vision to revolutionise transportation, and with it came the invention of the automobile. Before engineering the car of his dreams, he dove deep into researching who would buy it, digging up what they could spend, and learning what features they desired. When the Model T rolled out, Ford had the perfect recipe for success: knowledge of who would purchase it, what features they'd love and how much they'd pay. Additionally, Ford Motor Company revolutionised the car industry with their assembly line, allowing for the speedy production of automobiles! Through exceptional treatment of staff, Ford maintained both its loyal workforce and renowned product quality. The ultimate efficiency was born thanks to this outstanding combination! Critical brainstorming at Ford Motor Company transformed problem-solving in the business arena, giving customers solutions before they knew they needed them, which is an excellent application of what Socrates advocated.

The human touch for better credibility

How do you build better credibility? Do you achieve it by spending lots of money on advertisements and employing more workforce or by media attention? The answer is incredibly simple, and yet entrepreneurs struggle with it – the human touch! This is where I am sure that artificial intelligence fails miserably. The human angle is very important in our day-to-day life as well as in our business decisions. Whether it be stakeholders, clients, partners or team members, it is necessary to build connections that appeal to human nature and have the element of relatability to it.

Aristotle's Nichomachean Ethics supports the importance of using one's reason and humanising the work environment. The workplace can be a place of dialogue that allows employees to express themselves freely. Edward Deci and Richard Ryan's Self-Determination Theory, which relates employee motivation to improved performance, takes great inspiration from Aristotle's teachings. Results suggest that satisfying an employee's three psychological needs of autonomy, competence, and relatedness through growth opportunities, incentives, involvement in activities, and respect for their labour leads to stronger and more content teams, which ultimately correlates to higher productivity among entrepreneurial groups.

Lowry, in a study of Xenophonian entrepreneurship models, was accurate in noting that recent economic studies have re-emphasised the importance of the human factor in economic activity. Taking cues from the most successful businesses in America, one study recommends to entrepreneurs that they recognise individuals—as opposed to investments and automation—as their top factor of productivity enhancement.

Founders of many successful businesses have been remarkable employers as they have taken good care of their human resources as well as the sentiments of the customers.

HJ Heinz strived to make the workplace a clean, safe, and comfortable place for all employees, especially the women workforce—a stark contrast to the unhealthy and cruel working conditions of the factories of that time.

He also ensured recreational allowances with reasonable working hours, wage raises, sick leaves, and medical benefits. Moreover, he just did not delegate tasks to his managers but went to even the lower-level factory workers to note down their complaints against the management that he took care of personally. He was interested in the welfare of his employees, urging them to abandon bad habits and lead a 'righteous life.'

Source: https://profectusmag.com/american-original-hj-heinz/

He displayed the same compassion for his packaging for its potential customers by rolling out designs for bottles that were easy to pack, stored and clearly labelled. These were sanitised transparent bottles so that customers could buy them with confidence as, at that time, a lot of people were wary of packaged foods owing to a wave of contaminated food products in the market that was making a lot of people ill. Heinz ultimately became synonymous with purity when the company teamed up with a scientist from the US Agriculture

Department to support the Pure Food and Drug Act. It was one of the first companies to encourage the general public to take a tour of the factories—a wonderful move that ensured the faith of the customers.

Break away from the herd: A Neitzchian perspective

Nietzsche was known as a German writer, thinker, and cultural analyst. His ideas on aesthetics, truth, language, morality, history, nihilism, power, cultural theory, consciousness and the meaning of existence have had a great influence on Western philosophy.[xx, xxi, xxii, xxiii, xxiv, xxv]

Source: https://iveybusinessjournal.com/the-nietzsche-school-of-management/

Friedrich Nietzsche's thought focuses on freeing oneself from the collective thoughts of society because this kind of thinking can be detrimental, inevitably bringing displeasure to one's existence. Those who remain ingratiated in the herd mentality tend to become bored and uninspired, unable to capitalise on opportunities or progress professionally.

> "You have no idea what you are experiencing; you run through life as if you were drunk and once in a while fall down a staircase."

You can't copy your way to success. Instead, you need to develop a unique viewpoint. He suggests seeking isolation in order to generate something unique and uncover personal objectives instead. He states that this method could make us more self-sufficient and independent.

According to Nietzsche, every human being desires their own citadel and privacy, which helps them to remain far from the majority. He also believed that greatness includes desiring solitude, distinctiveness, and the ability to live alone [*auf-eigne-Faust-leben-müssen*]. According to Nietzsche, another trait championed by great men is being wholly committed and engrossed in duties, responsibilities, and projects.

"What is noble?" he pondered in a *Nachlass* note of 1888. His answer: "That one instinctively seeks heavy responsibilities." But this does not mean that we seek out responsibilities and tasks arbitrarily. Nietzsche states that a great person is capable of putting logic into all of their actions and being able to withstand temptations and reject anything trivial. Nietzsche occasionally alludes to this trait as having a "style" in "character."

In 1889, he released *Twilight of the Idols, or How to Philosophize with a Hammer*, which gives insight into his thinking as demonstrated by this quote:

"With the unknown, one is confronted with danger, discomfort, and care; the first instinct is to abolish these painful states. First principle: any explanation is better than none. Because it is fundamentally just our desire to be rid of an unpleasant uncertainty, we are not very particular about how we get rid of it: the first interpretation that explains the unknown in familiar terms feels so good that one 'accepts it as true.' The 'why' shall, if at all possible, result not in identifying the cause for its own sake but in identifying a cause that is comforting, liberating, and relieving. A second consequence of this need is that we identify as a cause something already familiar or experienced, something already inscribed in memory. Whatever is novel or strange or never before experienced is excluded."

This is worthy of reflection from the entrepreneurial perspective. Stressed-out CEOs wanting to explain why sales are plunging often choose the easy explanations rather than investigating the complex and nuanced factors and comfort themselves while the actual problem is undetected. There are several reasons why this could be happening in a company, like marketing strategies, competitor landscape, product quality, blockage of funds, manufacturing issues, and employee dissatisfaction, but instead of looking into these, maybe the senior executive would just blast the head of the marketing because that's the easiest thing to do! Takes the stress off, too!

"What does not kill me makes me stronger" is one of Friedrich Nietzsche's most popularly cited quotes (though it frequently gets misquoted). Business leaders should use their mistakes to become stronger. More often than not, the bigger your mistake, the more you learn. Being outdone by a competitor or fighting amongst business partners can be beneficial in pushing you to get revenge—though in a positive, productive way. Losing and failing can be beneficial in the long run, as they lead to learning experiences and eventual success.

Nietzsche famously posed his concept of the '*ubermensch*' in 1883 in his book *Writing*. There needs to be chaos within oneself to create a dancing star." Entrepreneurs need to be constantly thinking out of the box, churning out new ideas constantly within themselves through keen observation and application of concepts rather than involving themselves in too much competition and pursuing trends blindly.

Highly successful companies have their own unique approaches to corporate culture. Take Zappos, the fashion retailer, for example. They have employee benefits like free food, wellness services, and shoe-shining. The unique culture they've cultivated at their company is worth the price they pay for it as it attracts a better quality of employees and work. Allowing even the most unconventional solutions can help to generate more innovative problem-solving ideas. Take Netflix as an example. By imagining a different approach to the conventional video store setup of borrowing and overdue charges, they made something that quickly became popular around the world. What innovative solutions could you come up with if you don't limit yourself to existing ideas?

Tech behemoth Apple is known for its mantra: "Think different."

Therefore, follow Nietzsche's advice and don't be afraid to take risks; it can help make you stand out from the competition in a positive manner.

Obstacle to actionable solution

> The impediment to action advances action. What stands in the way becomes the way?"
> —Marcus Aurelius

We all have, at some point, admired pearls, right? These lustrous beauties have been considered by French psychologist Boris

Cyrulnik as symbols of how tuning our response and attitude towards obstacles is necessary for development and creation. The oyster, in response to its irritation with a grain of sand stuck inside its shell, produces a substance that ultimately solidifies into a pearl! This, my friends, is how entrepreneurs should convert obstacles into solutions, and there are plenty of examples in history to learn from.

As an entrepreneur, the ability to confront hardships makes you stronger; obstacles can be seen as chances, and considering how small your business is helps control your ego and keeps it in perspective. The obstacles you go through in life shape your identity! Greek scholar Onasander, in his writing *The General*, states that a leader should be quick to think and act in times of uncertainty, and if an unexpected problem arises, they should come up with equally swift solutions.[xxvi] Marcus Aurelius, in his book *Meditations,* has given many examples wherein he finds that all the obstacles lead him to a new successful direction.

Do any of you remember reading about Hercules during your school days? Is that correct? Just imagine what would have happened to Hercules if there was no lion, hydra, stag, or boar and no evil perpetrators for him to stop. No adversities to face or defeat? If those challenges had not been present, what would he have done? Will he be known in history as the mighty "Hercules"? Are you familiar with the chronicles of Alexander the Great[27] or King Cyrus the Great of Persia?[xxvii] How about the infamous conflict between King Xerxes of Persia and King Leonidas of Sparta in the Battle of Thermopylae? Without overcoming all their obstacles, who would've remembered them today? As entrepreneurs, you will often encounter make-or-break moments in your business journey. While ancient warfare is no longer a reality, the business landscape is still an unpredictable battlefield, with competitors lurking around every corner. By learning from ancient warfare, you can be armed with timeless wisdom to keep going and fortify your courage and tenacity.

We should consider that at the core of the inability of entrepreneurs to tackle issues in the business world is the fear of the complex. They envision the problems to be too complicated to solve and buckle under immense pressure. Here, a powerful disentangling technique is the "first principles" concept introduced by Aristotle that advocates the breaking down of complex problems, examining the components for step-by-step resolution and then reassembling to see the complete jig-saw. The term "first principles" has also been used in quantum mechanics and simulations while devising algorithms for solving the motion and structure of complex biomolecules. Nothing is insurmountable. Breaking down a large task into smaller, achievable components may facilitate successful completion. Tycoons like Elon Musk and Netflix CEO Reed Hastings swear by this systematic approach to tackling challenges. Henry Ford approached every obstacle with a simple yet profound understanding that there are no big problems but lots of little ones, solving which can pave the way for success. This was the mantra guiding his reign at Ford Motor Company. Ford's journey to business success began with one small step at a time—getting creative inputs, designing an amazing product, setting the perfect price point, and bringing it to life with our killer advertising strategy!

Another virtue preached by Aristotle that is thought to enhance skills and reflexes in the face of adversities is experiential learning and practical wisdom that never leaves an individual stranded but equips him/her with critical thinking skills to handle any situation.

In fact, taking a cue from Athenian entrepreneurs, one should be on the lookout for potential opportunities that others have missed due to certain hindrances and capitalise on them! For example, in Xenophon's book Oeconomicus, the author describes how Ischomachus' father bought poorly tended land and increased its value by properly tending it and selling it for a higher profit. Xenophon noted that capitalists were reluctant to risk their hard-earned money on mining investments, making it difficult for them to invest in the industry. He recommended that in these instances, having a finance management system would be able to evenly allocate the risks and profits.

Aristotle, in his political treatise, *Politics*, also recalled the case of Thales, the first Greek philosopher. Drawing on his expertise in forecasting and astrological mathematics, he invested in off-season olive presses before everybody else. This increased demands during the olive oil-pressing season, and he was able to sell it to peasants at a higher price later. Thales achieved this feat after being challenged to show that one could become wealthy and successful with the use of philosophy!

To put our point across effectively, let us examine the story behind Nestle. This company has transformed its challenges into profitable solutions. Henri Nestlé, the founder, started out by addressing the problem of milk storage and transportation in the pre-refrigeration era by producing better quality condensed milk as well as alternative supplements to breast milk. When World War I began, several companies began to experience losses as demand for products was high, but supplies were scarce. Nestle refused to back down, shifting its focus on production centres in Europe to those in the US and Australia, and as a result, production nearly doubled even during and after the war. The brand even transformed the problems of other manufacturers into solutions! The Brazilian government asked the company if they could do something about the excess of coffee that they were producing, and pat came to the answer! Nescafe, our favourite instant coffee, was born.

Group of soldiers have coffee and doughnuts on their way to their station in England, 1944.
Source: https://rarehistoricalphotos.com/detroit-early-1940s/

The true potential of this drink came to light when the Second World War isolated the production centres in Europe and Australia, and Nestle expanded its distribution to developing countries. As soon as America joined the war, Nescafe was projected as the preferred drink for these soldiers during the difficult times.

Nestle soon acquired many companies and announced mergers over the years, maintaining its innovative strategies for providing sustainable solutions, which helped it become a household name.

The next brand that remained calm in the face of adversity and changed its strategies for the better was Samsung. When Samsung phones started to catch fire when left unchecked, the company incurred considerable criticism due to the perilous issue. With persistence, Samsung was able to bounce back. The initial step was to eliminate all existing phones. To rectify the issue, the company issued a recall of the Note 7, halted all sales and shipments, reimbursed users, and provided exchanges for the phones. Sadly, the replacements for faulty devices had the same problem, too, so Samsung recalled them as well.

The company accepted full accountability for their issue. The research team was comprehensive in their testing, as they tried phones and batteries under extreme conditions to pinpoint the issue. After the Samsung phone debacle, they acknowledged where the issues arose; the batteries were larger than their appropriate casings and that caused them to overheat. Additionally, they also declared the implementation of a quality assurance program as well as other safety features.

Samsung attempted to gain back the trust of customers by reminding them why they should be loyal to the brand. The company underwent an internal culture shift due to its brand identity, which appeared emotionally distant. As a response, the company created a tagline—"*Do What You Can't*"—in order to create a unified purpose among their consumers. The new campaign focused on the relationship between phone usage and content creators. To increase their popularity, they hired the famous YouTuber Casey Neistat and showcased their new brand in an Oscar commercial.

This helped Samsung bounce back, and customers were glad that the company had taken steps to not only identify and acknowledge their issues but also rectify all previous mistakes.

The power of strategic brand dominance: Be like Julius Caesar

Well, dear readers, here I am taking a small risk. Julius Caesar is a bit controversial figure in history, but I love his example and therefore would like to add him to this book. Julius Caesar was a powerful figure in Roman history who established himself firmly in the hearts and minds of generations owing to his flamboyant yet strategic decisions, public speaking prowess and spreading his influence through public shows of valour and entertainment.[27][xxviii, xxix, xxx]

The iconic phrase, *veni, vidi, Vici* (I came, I saw, I conquered) is renowned in history. In 47 BC, Julius Caesar spoke the famous phrase for the first time after his success against Pharnaces II of Pontus in The Battle of Zela. The expression ended up becoming a symbol of Caesar's strength and ambition while also imparting the lesson that even a powerful leader can be succinct when it comes to describing their accomplishments. Caesar's words showed how quickly and effectively he conquered Pharnaces II; after arriving at the battle and analysing the situation, he was able to easily defeat his opponent.

Apart from being historically influential, this quote is also an important reminder that there are times when simplicity yields more effective communication. Through the use of only three words, Caesar conveyed his success succinctly without wasting

time on elaborate detailing or superfluous words. His meaningful words still remain relevant today and provide a great example for anyone wanting to communicate effectively.

Plutarch's narrative about Julius Caesar being abducted by pirates is a remarkable demonstration of his brave spirit and determination. Upon being asked for ransom by the pirates, Caesar laughed and offered to pay them twice as much. He followed up with an even more daring promise: that he would track them down and kill them after he was released. Staying true to his promise, Caesar assembled a fleet, located the pirates in order and killed them to take his revenge.

In Roman tradition, deserters from the military were typically punished regardless of their relationship to the leadership. Caesar personally undertook this challenge. His men saw this as a demonstration that he was willing to do whatever was considered the most difficult. In his time as dictator, he took a firm stance against those who had been involved in bribery and extortion, punishing them harshly. The most effective leaders act logically and don't influence their choices with emotions of bias. In his writing, Caesar once noted that "in war, important outcomes arise from small causes." This was reflective of his leadership style in warfare; Caesar took great care in analysing every detail of a battle prior to it taking place and considered every seemingly insignificant factor. Based on his own experience with them, he carefully chose each soldier to serve in leadership positions within his legions. In every war Caesar took part in, he emerged victorious.

In the year 52 BC, a local ruler from Gaul called Vercingetorix became the leader of his people, the Arverni. Famous for unifying the French tribes to oppose Julius Caesar, Vercingetorix would have been triumphant if not for Caesar's inventive tactics. At the last battle of Alesia, Vercingetorix had built defences to block the Romans and give his reinforcements time to come and ambush Caesar's soldiers from behind. Understanding the difficulty of the circumstance, Caesar ordered siege fortifications to be constructed for himself. In an effort to gain an upper hand against his adversaries, Caesar constructed walls on either side of his soldiers. Despite the odds stacked against him, his plan went off splendidly. Caesar implemented a dual-wall defence, which successfully kept enemy reinforcements at bay and saved his army from potential defeat. In spite of Vercingetorix successfully rallying the Gaul tribes against Caesar, he still lost in the ultimate battle.

The whole message which I want to convey here is that in business, not only do you need courage but also firm and decisive actions. Not only sometimes your actions have to be bold but also innovative in order to make an impact in the world. So, had Steve Jobs decided to make another keypad phone, we don't know if the iPhone would have made a mark on its consumers. But when the iPhone was launched without any physical keypad, it altogether changed the world of mobile computing.

Morally sound business practices for long-term success

To most entrepreneurs, the business world seems like a jungle; you either survive or perish and must relentlessly keep moving forward. According to Cornwall and Naughton in their book *Bringing Your Business to Life*, the majority of the ethical issues blighting businesses currently are not caused by malicious people but by those with technical and financial expertise who disregard moral values while trying to achieve economic objectives.

Aristotle wrote: *"We are not studying to know what virtue is but to become good; otherwise, there would be no profit in it."*

In both *Rhetoric* and *Nicomachean Ethics*, Aristotle was adamant that unethical or illegal profit to be made through means such as piracy should not be condoned. The Greeks viewed certain actions such as stealing, not paying what was promised in a contract (as Hyperides mentioned in his text *Against Athenogenes*), trespassing another's property, making excessive or immoral profit off someone else and not providing fair wages as illegal and unjust.

Hyperides noted in his book *Euxenippus* that some businessmen argued that by taking away the output of workers' labour, they were creating resources for the city; in actuality, this action set up economic difficulties for the future. Additionally, private enterprises often gain unfair profits from exploiting consumers through monopolisation. Lysias condemned retail traders for engaging in unfair practices, such as buying corn at a low price and then monopolising the market by selling it for a higher price.

(a)   (b)

(Sourced from a: modification of "Aristotle Altemps Inv8575" by "Jastrow"/Wikimedia Commons, Public Domain; credit b: modification of "Aristotelis De Moribus ad Nicomachum" by "Aavindraa"/Wikimedia Commons, Public Domain)

Customers today are now more knowledgeable and influential than ever before, expecting companies to be honest and conscious of their actions. For example, adhering to its mantra of "radical transparency," US fashion e-tailer Everlane started offering Transparency Tours in 2015 to give customers a look at the production process of its products in factory facilities across the United States. The company opened an 'Open House' pop-up in New York showcasing its products with infographics on their backgrounds and hosting events with ethical food companies.

Surveys demonstrate that 55% of people from 60 countries are willing to pay more for products and services from companies that prioritise long-term, positive social and ecological impact (Nielsen 2014). In this context, it is interesting to note that The Body Shop, a cosmetics and skin care company, has for a long time used social and environmental campaigns to market its business. It established opposition to animal testing in cosmetics as a core value.

Ethical scandals in the business world can create a strong negative impression of a corporation, leaving employees and customers with an unfavourable opinion of the company's moral posture. A company's reaction to small-scale ethical dilemmas and scandals is are indicator of their core values and practices. Ethical misconduct, negligence, or interference from third parties that damage a business's reputation may be considered a corporate scandal. Through this, we can observe signs of "creative" accounting, fraudulent business conduct, data leakage or anything that harms the environment. Business ethics revolves around the industry, its practices, interactions with customers, earnings and expenditure, as well as corporate regulations. To ensure customers are pleased with their experience at the workplace, management must prioritise business ethics as well as quality control as a key component of the company.

After all, as Henry Ford once remarked, *"Quality means doing it right even when no one is looking."*

The downfall of Enron and the conviction of a few of its Board members made headlines as one of the most striking examples of ethics violations in recent memory.

Bernie Madoff was an American financier who ran a **multibillion-dollar Ponzi scheme** that is considered the largest financial fraud of all time. Similarly, WorldCom, which was then the U.S.'s second-biggest long-distance telecommunications organisation, was involved in a scandal. Lehman Brothers, Theranos, Wirecard, etc., are all examples of companies that lost their core values and got into greed and fraud. We have so many examples from India, like Satyam, Sahara India, ILFS, Yes Bank, Videocon, etc., which are classic examples of downfall when companies lose their path of ethics.

Source: © Adam Rountree/Getty Images. https://www.ft.com/content/fb2366ff-fe13-441d-998d-3dedc4110491

One example I would like to go in more detail. A few years ago, the US Environmental Protection Agency exposed that Volkswagen had been cheating on emissions tests, sparking what we now refer to as the VW emissions scandal. Subsequently, it was discovered that the company had been outfitting its diesel cars with what some industry onlookers called 'defeat devices' whose software detected when the vehicles were subjected to laboratory testing and activated controls that cut down on nitrogen emissions. It appeared as if the cars met the standards of the agency, but while they were on the road, they actually emitted nitrogen dioxide at a rate that was up to 40x more than the limit. This finding sparked investigations around the globe, and some reports suggest up to 11 million cars were affected by the issue.

It was a similar issue that led to the downfall of GM Motors. The GM debacle took a wild turn when the faulty ignition switch reared its head during a fateful test drive of the Saturn Ion. Upon further investigation, it was discovered that a multitude of other models were plagued with the same pesky glitch.

The company's swift action would have made a real difference in mitigating any potential harm. Imagine the headline: "Safety First: Company Takes Immediate Steps to Address Production Issue." It could have raised trust among the customers, but no! Despite the repercussions of its faulty ignition systems, the production line persisted in churning out defective products, ultimately resulting in devastating consequences.

It is important for entrepreneurs to not get carried away by utopian dreams and risk their reputations by indulging in morally corrupt practices for short-term gains. Instead, choose to do what keeps your company safe. Have a long-term vision and goals. Choose what is ethical and right, and you will not regret it.

Key Insights for Ancipreneurs:

Entrepreneurs should harness the power of facts and brand imaging to attract customers. They might use pathos to evoke positive emotions in their audience, such as curiosity or enthusiasm. Lastly, they might employ ethos to build credibility with the audience by showcasing their intelligence and good intentions. Remember Aristotle and his valuable advice!

- Connect to your audiences with irrefutable arguments about their pain points and craft brands that they would like to associate themselves with throughout their lifetime. Proper market research, analysis of trends and customised approaches for brand communications can uplift the credibility of your enterprise. Dig deep and find out what your target market craves: it's time to get creative! Ask questions and seek answers, like Arjun in the "Gita."

- Executives today need to be networking with key influencers who have different outlooks in order to survive in the business world. By doing so, their own thinking can be expanded, and a new perspective gained. Connecting with these people can take place in various ways like think tanks, roundtables, or other such opportunities. Executives can gain valuable insight and devise creative strategies for their business by networking and influencing with clear communication.

- Executives must remember to follow in the footsteps of Julius Caesar and be willing to take risks if they want to succeed. But it's crucial to evaluate risks before taking action. Leaders must weigh the possible advantages of their decisions and be willing to bear the outcomes. Executives can make sure that their business succeeds when transitioning by taking an informed approach to risk-taking.

So, let me share you here a small activity to see your understanding of the concepts:

Activity 1: My shoemaking career started in my mother's washroom, located in a small Bavarian town in Germany. It was at this place that I started making and designing shoes, and I wanted to make the perfect sports shoe for athletes. While many other footwear manufacturers were present, I wanted to be different. I reached out to target customers and interacted with them about their aspirations, requirements, and trouble spots. My company soon began to be recognised as a premium sports shoe brand, and there was no looking back after that. Who am I? Which ancipreneurial principles did I apply?

Write your answer here.

Trivia: Yes, you guessed it right! This was none other than Adi Dassler, the founder of Adidas. According to Adidas's website, a major contributing factor

to *Adi Dassler's success was his commitment to listening to athletes and responding immediately to their needs with improvements or inventions. This led the most talented athletes of the time to trust in him and his company from the beginning.*

Activity 2: World War II has just ended, and as a Japanese, you are feeling the pinch of the scarcity of basic materials for sustenance. Your immense interest in electronics prompts you to endeavour to make tape recorders, but you lack resources and financial support. What would you do?

You have a dream of revamping your company, Tokyo Telecommunications Co. and finding American investors, but you're not having any breakthrough. An agent from the Bulova watch company shows interest in the mini transistor radios and gives you an order of 10,000 units with the condition that they would be marketed with the Bulova brand name. This is a huge investment that finds support from your company's board, and they pressure you into accepting the offer. What should you do?

What ancipreneurial principles from this chapter would you apply in these two instances?

Write your answer here:

Trivia: *This is the story of Akio Morita, the entrepreneur who wanted his company to transform into an international brand.*

He transformed his obstacles into actionable solutions by ingeniously cutting mimeograph paper into narrow strips with blades. To craft the magnetic coating, a batch of oxalic ferrite powder was cooked up on a skillet that transformed into ferric oxide and painted on the strips. The audio might not have been top-notch, but hey - it did the job! The beginnings of Sony might have been humble, but his endeavours soon began to take shape. When Bulova company gave him the offer and urgent telegrams began to arrive from Sony's board, he turned it down. This was tough as the amount was more than the entire capital fund of Sony. But for him, the brand was everything, and he wanted his products to exhibit brand dominance internationally. This would later be referred to as one of his best business decisions ever!

Activity 3: Imagine this paradox – You've just received the Ernest and Young Entrepreneur of the Year Award,' the 'Golden Peacock Award' for Corporate Accountability, and MZ Consult for being a 'Leader in Indian Corporate Governance and Accountability and yet you have hoodwinked corporate audits, by faking customer identities, salaries of employees as well as having sources of income. Which business lesson from this chapter would you apply here to check yourself? Write your answer here:

Trivia: This is the story of Satyam – one of India's best corporate frauds with several hundred crores of scammed money. Charges of data theft by the World Bank, lack of proper documentation and misappropriation of funds levelled at founder Ramalinga Raju and brothers took a toll on the shares of Satyam till its takeover by Tech Mahindra.

CHAPTER 3

STOICISM IN ANCIENT ROME: FOUR TAKEAWAYS FOR BUDDING ANCIPRENEURS

The school of Stoicism was established in Athens by Zeno of Citium during the early third century BC. The name of the philosophy, Stoicism, comes from the Greek word "stoa," meaning porch. That was where Zeno first taught his students. This belief system maintains that virtue leads to joy, and it's our views of things—not the actual things themselves—that create tension in our lives. Stoicism is an ancient school of Western philosophy centred on the idea that we should use reason to control our own emotions, responses, and perspectives when faced with external events. It encourages mindfulness, resilience, creativity and more to allow individuals to thrive and experience true happiness. Stoicism has had a massive impact on Western thought and is known for its straightforward, down-to-earth attitude compared to other philosophical schools, which get lost in long and complicated discussions. President Barack Obama is often noted for his stoic demeanour—much like Cato the Younger, an influential political figure heavily influenced by stoicism.

Adopting a stoic mindset can help you turn negative emotions into a broader view of the situation and encourage you to maintain the proper mental attitude. Its core is about taking charge of the things that you can control and letting go of the rest. To be successful in this, you must be aware and have control of your emotions and thoughts rather than getting lost in them. Stoic exercises, such as imagining we are in unfortunate and impoverished situations, help teach us that the worst-case scenario may not be as bad as we think. This is incredibly beneficial for business.[xxxi, xxxii, xxxiii, xxxiv, xxxv, xxxvi, xxxvii, xxxviii, xxxix, xl, xli]

Numerous famous minds in history cherished Stoicism and even purposely sought it out, including Theodore Roosevelt, George Washington, Eugène Delacroix, Ralph Waldo Emerson, Walt Whitman, Frederick the Great, Matthew Arnold, Adam Smith, Immanuel Kant, Thomas Jefferson, Ambrose Bierce, and William Alexander Percy.

An example of this is George Washington, who was likely exposed to Stoicism in his teenage years through a family he knew. It is uncertain how much Washington practised Stoicism. However, he did stage a theatrical play for his army about Cato, a famous Ancient Stoic philosopher. Additionally, he was reported to be in the habit of recollecting Stoic aphorisms and wise quotes from philosophers. Based on this information and Washington's renowned composure in difficult situations, it can be inferred that he used Stoic tactics to manage adversity. Similarly, James Mattis followed some of these Stoic principles during his illustrious time in the military. During his service in the military, Mattis had a well-known passion for reading. He drew inspiration from many of history's wise authors, but he kept one book with him wherever he went and urged all Americans to read it - the concepts given by Epictetus.

Let us have a look at the various lessons that can inspire entrepreneurs from the teachings of ancient Roman stoics.

"Memento mori" and *"Premeditatio malorum"*

Anxiety never bodes well for entrepreneurs who are always trying to cope with lost opportunities and brood over how things are not going their way instead of looking within and planning ahead. By practising memento mori, which translates from Latin to "remember we must die," we can gain a deeper understanding of life and live out every moment more purposefully. While it may seem a bit grim to focus on the end of our days, recognising our mortality helps us to make the most of the limited time we have. While the world is focused on prolonging life, becoming more familiar with death can help us live fuller metaphorical lives. By giving our lives meaning and purpose, we can make them more meaningful and fulfilling, avoiding an empty or monotonous life filled with activities that don't have any real significance. Drawing on its theoretical foundations, empirical studies, and practical applications, existential positive psychology challenges us to bravely confront the inevitability of death in order to live with greater purpose and vigour—to strive for a meaningful life. Since people began writing and reading, literature on death themes has existed. More than four thousand years ago, *The Epic of Gilgamesh* told the tale of a hero's journey as he comes to terms with death—of his friend's and his own.

Are you aware that simulating scenarios and doing 'what-if' analysis is an essential element in teaching management students and even boardrooms of the corporate world? These scenarios often include the most pessimistic outcomes, which are meant to respond to unpredictable events from competition and failure. The stoic concept of 'premeditatio malorum' involves picturing the worst-case scenario every day and preparing for it in order to face the possible adversities that come with being an entrepreneur. Let me give you the example of Clive Woodward, the former coach of England's World Cup-winning rugby team, who was famous for his attention to detail. He used to prepare for every possible scenario—from player injury to weather changes and even streakers on the field. Nothing caught him off guard. In his own words, "There shouldn't be anything in sport or business that you haven't thought about." Woodward's approach proves that preparation is key to success, both on and off the field. Similarly, Michael Jordan insisted on training players with the toughest of conditions to prepare them for the worst, believing that a little discomfort and pain in the training period would acclimatise them to rise up to challenges on-field. To put it simply, the best way to approach entrepreneurial life these days is to "hope for the best and plan for the worst."

These two concepts help achieve a 'zen' state supported by the Greek terms of

- Apatheia is the condition of being free from or unaffected by emotion or suffering.
- Ataraxis is a peaceful mental state where your emotions cannot be disturbed.
- Autarkeis is the ability to remain internally independent.

We end this section with Epictetus's befitting quote, *"Instead of averting your eyes from the painful events of life, look at them squarely and contemplate them often. By facing the realities of death, infirmity, loss, and disappointment, you free yourself of illusions and false hopes and you avoid miserable, envious thoughts."*

The mechanics of control – A multi-pronged perspective

> "*We control our reasoned choice and all acts that depend on that moral will. What's not under our control are the body and any of its parts, our possessions, parents, siblings, children, or country —anything with which we might associate.*" —**Epictetus,** *Discourses*

Entrepreneurs frequently contend with many sources of pressure, such as deadlines, conflicting obligations, investor desires and client grievances. That pressure can lead to stress for some people. It is widely known that too much stress is not only detrimental to our health but also negatively impacts the productivity and profitability of businesses. On the other hand, some people are able to handle pressure without becoming excessively stressed. Understanding the things we can and cannot control, or as Epictetus put it, "externals," brings us to only focusing on the "internals," which helps save much time and also creates a healthier work environment.

According to Coventry (2016), by incorporating Stoicism—a line of philosophy from Aurelius, Epictetus, and Seneca—into their daily routines, entrepreneurs can develop the mental resilience needed to persevere through failures and tough times in business. Doing so will help them create clear goals while staying brave amidst life's unexpected twists. According to Epictetus, the main goal in life is to differentiate between what we can control and what is out of our reach.

What we can control is our temptation. This temptation can emerge in the most basic of instincts like procrastination or whiling away time. Stoics like Seneca, Epictetus, and Marcus Aurelius always stressed the importance of the time. As entrepreneurs, we often wile away a lot of time talking and debating instead of taking action. In certain circumstances, it can be very damaging for businesses; for example, in marketplaces, you must work quickly to stay ahead of the competition. If we delay our actions, it tends to cause us great levels of stress, which can then lead to wrong decisions with disastrous consequences. Fearful panic, coupled with anger and frustration, can be detrimental to any entrepreneur's success. According to Seneca, the well-known Stoic philosopher, anger is the worst vice and the most destructive emotion. In his essay, *The Shortness of Life*, he emphasises that life isn't as short as it seems, but our continual wasting of time through unnecessary procrastination prevents us from achieving our life goals, thus making us age quicker from the burden of failure.

Journaling for entrepreneurial success

By recording his daily experiences via journaling, the ancient Stoic king Marcus Aurelius was able to find purpose and use it to vanquish procrastination and idleness from his consciousness. In fact, his book Meditations was his own personal clarity!

Not only does putting a business idea on paper make it feel more realistic, but it also allows for the concept to develop and expand. Reflection involves carefully considering your observations, experiences and alternative interpretations with the goal of learning from them to make better decisions in the future. Studies show that those who take the time to reflect tend to be happier and more successful than those who don't. It's logical. Those who perform well and are content with life use their errors to grow.

There are boundaries to your thinking. Our brain can only store a limited number of feelings and thoughts, not all of them helpful. Keeping a journal is a great way to boost productivity, as it allows your thoughts and ideas to develop without the burden of unnecessary concerns. Furthermore, journaling is also beneficial for examining whether or not your business dreams will succeed, allowing you to realistically assess if they are feasible. You might think your plan is perfect when discussing it with enthusiastic friends or colleagues. Rather than having to worry about other people's judgement, journaling can be an honest way to recognise the shortcomings of a business plan.

> *"I will keep constant watch over myself and—most usefully—will put each day up for review. For this is what makes us evil—that none of us looks back upon our own lives. We reflect upononly that which we are about to do."*

Seneca, in a letter to his elder brother Novatus, points out a useful exercise he learned from another well-known philosopher and that our plans for the future are rooted in the past. Every evening, he would reflect on eliminating any bad habits he had developed throughout the day by asking himself variations of this question: What unhealthy habit did I address today? How can I improve? Was I justified in my actions? How can I become better?

Do you know that HJ Heinz, the founder of Heinz Ketchup Industries, used to maintain a lot of notebooks on-farm practices, harvests, seasons, production and sales data since he was a teenager till the end of his business career? He carried his notebooks everywhere that he went, filling them on competition research, market analysis, measurements, and travel insights.

Another example is that of the great inventor Thomas Alva Edison. Edison was very careful and attentive when it came to his planning. He used to create precise sketches of his concepts and innovations. Additionally, he maintained precise documentation of his entrepreneurial pursuits. Edison began jotting down his revolutionary ideas and experiments in his trusty notebooks at the young age of 20, paving the way for ground-breaking innovations that would change the world as we knew it.

Source: Wikimedia Commons. Original picture from https://www.theatlantic.com/politics/archive/2011/04/picture-of-the-day-benjamin-franklins-daily-schedule/237615/

Entrepreneurs can journal about observations from meetings, suggestions to be considered, proposed roadmaps, elevator pitches, success and failure stories of businesses that impacted them, competitor research, time management, schedules, and so much more! One can also note what events contributed to or detracted from happiness. Before we conclude this section, take a look at a page from Benjamin Franklin's notebook. Do you see how maintaining a notebook helps with clarity of thought?

Innovate to raise the quality of the human cosmopolis

This viewpoint of universal brotherhood was perhaps adopted as part of Western philosophy by stoics [33,36]. For instance, Epictetus stated that we may be citizens of our land, but if we look at the bigger picture, we are also members "of the great city of gods and men." Another example is that of Marcus Aurelius, who loved his native city but kept reminding himself and others to love the world around him equally. Cyrus the Great was known to have used innovations like using a bigger wheelbase in his chariots or giving sudden surprise to his enemies by using elephants instead of camels. [5] Similarly, it is said that one of the key reasons for the success of Alexander in his wars was that King Philip II had developed "Sarissa," which helped and gave them an edge over other armies.

An engaging story of how a brand used innovation for welfare and increased its brand value is that of Procter & Gamble, who demonstrated the benefits of not letting a crisis suspend innovation, even during wartime. For example, during WWII, Procter & Gamble chemists conducted research on plastics using glycerine, cotton linters and soybeans—the same materials that were vital to the war effort—and kept using them for future products.

Prior to the start of WWII, P&G utilised its production capability and engineering know-how to diversify away from just consumer goods. Developing professional connections was a benefit. With its extensive connections in the industry and high-level personnel, P&G had access to people in the U.S. government. American government representatives saw that P&G's manufacturing and operational procedures could be used to load explosives as well as soap powder, so they collaborated with the company. This led to the Procter & Gamble Defence Corporation being established, which managed a shell-loading plant in Tennessee until 1941. After the attack on Pearl Harbor, production was increased, and other factories opened.

Let us examine another case study, and this time, let's immerse ourselves in nostalgia as we ponder over our favourite biscuit brand that's been around for. It stands out for innovation with a purpose. Not only has it catered to people of multiple demographics and adapted to changing markets and competition with dignity, but it has also lent its support to welfare programmes. The Indian government rolled out the *Center Meal Scheme* in 2010, delivering a nutritious cooked meal to college students with an aim to tackle malnutrition - an increasingly pressing problem in India and across the world. Britannia proudly deemed their involvement by providing specially enriched biscuits to kids, underscoring the power of social initiatives. To maximise its potential, the organisation strived to amp up the production and circulation of promotional items, transforming them into an established business entity.

amazon To further strengthen our idea of how innovation for quality can add credibility, we can examine the success story of Jeff Bezos and his empire of online retail business – Amazon. Amazon had humble beginnings from a garage in Seattle, where Jeff correctly identified the lack of access to books worldwide due to lack of stock and focussed on building the "Earth's biggest bookstore" so that readers all over the world had the option of choosing from over a million titles. It beat the competition owing to its customer-centric policies and constant innovation in terms of products (Kindle, Fire, Alexa, etc.) and experiences. Amazon soon expanded into selling music and household products, and the rest is history. Bezos once remarked that success isn't a straight path but an iterative process where one has to constantly invent, adapt, launch and keep repeating. What has worked in

Amazon's favour is the trust factor because all its innovations have been targeted at improving the quality and ease of shopping for customers.

An example of how stylish innovation transformed women's wear can be illustrated with the help of the story of Coco Chanel. When this fabulous pioneer of modern fashion entered the world in 1883, women were burdened with an array of outdated and uncomfortable layers of corsets and garters - relics from a bygone era that failed to meet the practical needs of today's women. With a keen eye for a problem, she spotted an answer and thus spawned her wonderful designs! With her revolutionary cosy sweaters, comfortable sailor frocks, breathable tunics, and stunning little black dress, she re-imagined fashion to celebrate the flair of menswear! Recognising an untapped market opportunity, she crafted stylish and comfortable clothes with added practicality—cue the Chanel suit skirts with special pockets to store cigarette cases—tailor-made for busy businesswomen.

One of the most successful businesses, Unilever, invests more than a billion euros a year in research and innovation, and its focus has always been branding itself as a company that cares about the health and safety of its customer base as well as about the environment. It has a claim to over 20,000 patents in processing, manufacturing and packaging. Unilever, which primarily started out as a soap manufacturer, has now diversified itself into a huge variety of products that have been designed from renewable components, are cruelty-free, environment-friendly and free from carcinogenic compounds. For example, by recycling plastic from bottles and packaging, Lipton bottles have been made from 100% PET (recycled plastic). Unilever comes up with special technologies to make its product shopping guilt-free and filled with confidence for the consumers—using plant-based moisturisers in Dove, biodegradable ultra-mild surfactants, patented silver technology in Lifebuoy replacing carbolic acid, salt-free soup stock cube in Knorr—these innovations are all targeted towards safe healthcare. As their company page claims, innovation for global sustainability has always been a core business strategy for them.

Building resilience

We all fear something, but there's something that anyone will admit—the fear of failure is ingrained within us. Not surprisingly, history has plenty of examples that, in particular, failed businessmen and entrepreneurs were not treated with kindness, which has led to this kind of conditioning. Whether it be Greece in 800 BC or ancient Italy and France, entrepreneurs who couldn't save their ventures either had to wear a basket or a green bonnet over their aces and sit for hours to showcase their failures or were paraded naked and their business details discussed amongst the onlookers. Thankfully, modern-day entrepreneurs do not have to face all this drama today, but what about social media? The slightest turbulence is noted, and the accounts are subjected to virtual persecution.

A constant undercurrent amidst monitoring stock market trends and managing meetings, production lines and client demands is the fear of failure. Here's where the teachings of philosophers like Zeno and Epictetus come in handy, as they have always been proponents of the theory that wanting to achieve supreme happiness is at the centre of all desires and fears. The only traits that can help achieve this state are learning to overcome psychological constraints through building resilience and a strong character.

If you're scared of rejection, think of Columbus. What would have happened if he had been stopped in his tracks by his own country's rejection? But did he give up? Absolutely not. He persistently pursued his dream and eventually convinced Spain's Queen Isabella to invest in his grand voyage! Drawing inspiration from within, Columbus held fast to his vision and never looked back. Crafting his marketing pitch, he weaved an enthralling narrative, building his team and seeking funds with each captivating chapter.

Let us take the case of Jack Ma, the founder of Alibaba Group and the first Chinese entrepreneur to be on the cover of Forbes magazine.

According to him, "Never give up. Today is hard, tomorrow will be worse, but the day after tomorrow will be sunshine." This has been seen in his life, where how, after numerous rejections, including those from Harvard and KFC, to name a few, he still utilised his skills and team-building strategy and leveraged his understanding of the market to build his business empire. With tons of optimism and the ability to face difficulties, he has paved the way for many budding entrepreneurs. In his words, "*We made more mistakes than anybody can imagine. We made mistakes in raising capital. We made mistakes in management. We made mistakes in HR.*" He recognises how failures are stepping stones to success, and one must build resilience against dwelling or brooding upon them but look forward to fresh starts.

Source: Getty Images (Bettmann (contributor)

Similarly, had Chester Carlton, the 'Xerox' man, given in to his poverty-stricken conditions and ill health and been intimidated by over twenty rejections, he would have never combined his passion for science and engineering to crack a real-life problem of offices and educational institutes worldwide. His xerography proposal was accepted by Battelle Optical Institute as well as Haloid Company. He also had the foresight to apply for intellectual property rights with his brand name, which soon came in handy when IBM came up with a competitor device, thanks to his previous collaborator, Otto Kornei.

Speaking of rejections, the founder of Canva, Melanie Perkins, was determined to create an affordable online design tool, but she encountered over 100 rejections before she eventually got her first investment three years into trying. Perkins attributed this investment to a change in how she pitched.

Now, she starts by introducing the relatable problem Canva is aiming to solve. During an interview with Inc. magazine, Perkins noted that many people are overwhelmed when they open up Photoshop, emphasising the importance of helping your audience understand not just the solution but also the underlying problem. Today, Canva has enabled 60 million customers across 190 countries to produce their own designs.

Key Insights for Ancipreneurs

- Deal with the emergency effectively, but also plan for what comes after the crisis. In order to come up with ideas, sometimes you need to create a solution for the issue. When they have the opportunity, they can then decide how to best implement short-term solutions in the current situation or whatever comes after that.
- Uncertainty accompanies every step of an entrepreneurial journey—be it at the innovation stage, while entering new markets or while starting new ventures. The "ancipreneur approach" advocates blending learnings from ancient philosophies to help both fresh entrants as well as seasoned players overcome their inner fears and develop cognitive skills crucial to risk management in business. Facing uncertainty with risk and consequence analysis is part and parcel of swimming in any trade, and one important trait of ancipreneurs is cultivating resilience and a calm demeanour akin to that of the stoics.
- Keeping up with journaling can spur new and helpful ideas when it comes to entrepreneurship, as well as help entrepreneurs have a better sense of direction.
- Adopting the values of ancient stoicism can not only promote objectivity and rational thinking amidst turmoil but also help tide over emotional upheavals that affect decision-making. A

good starting point for budding entrepreneurs to learn how to face challenges calmly is *Meditations* by Marcus Aurelius.

In fact, a famous quote from Aurelius was quoted by Arnold Schwarzenegger while addressing the uncertainties faced by graduates during the COVID-19 pandemic, "What stands in the way becomes the way." Indeed, impediments just make us stronger and better!

Author Tim Ferris, in his book *Tao of Seneca*, says:

> "...Stoicism has spread like wildfire throughout Silicon Valley and the NFL in the last five years, becoming a mental toughness training system for CEOs, founders, coaches, and players alike. Super Bowl champions like the Patriots and Seahawks have embraced Stoicism to make them better competitors. In my own life, the results have been incredible."

Activity 1: You thrive on creativity. You love designing characters and dream of seeing them on screen someday. Yet, creativity doesn't pay that well, as you find yourself eating dog food and facing rent issues. To top your woes, your contract with Universal Pictures is under dispute, and this causes you to lose control over your beloved first character, Ostwald, the Rabbit. Even MGM has rejected a cute mouse character you just designed because it feels that the women audience wouldn't warm up to it. You're exhausted but just wouldn't give up. You carry on and finally reach the screening of your film, and just to welcome people, you hire performers to act as puppets and wave at the audience. Turns out, before the screening, they have all stripped down and are drunkenly

swearing at the audience! Should you give up already? Write your answer below.

(Photo: Library of Congress, Prints & Photographs Division, photograph by Harris & Ewing)

Trivia: Behold the failure story of Walt Disney! He faced numerous failures and non-acceptance of his vision for characters, but Mickey Mouse and so many other cartoon characters are still loved across the world. So, giving up is never an option! In 1957, Walt Disney famously said: "All the adversity I've had in my life, all my troubles and obstacles, have strengthened me... You may not realise it when it happens, but a kick in the teeth may be the best thing in the world for you."

Activity 2: Imagine yourself as an entrepreneur who has failed at seventeen companies out of the twenty that you have founded. You receive a phone call for an urgent board meeting, and you find out that you just lost 9 million dollars today because of a shareholder's losses. What would you do?

Trivia: This is a real-life situation that entrepreneur, podcaster, and venture capitalist author James Altucher faced. He applied 'Memento Mori' and, after a second of panic, took a deep breath and focussed on what he still had and was doing well. When he did an internal check of all the activities he did for self-care, spirituality, creativity and taking care of his loved ones, he arrived at the conclusion that he felt alive and that a monetary loss could change his bank account but not his story!

Activity 3: You've just learnt to make confectionery and are over the moon about it. At the age of eighteen, you start your own candy shop, but in just five years, it closes down! Then, you improve upon your skills and learn the art of making caramel. You launch two more businesses in New York and Chicago, but these fail as well. Things are not looking better at all. Should you continue or think of something else?

Trivia: We wouldn't have experienced the magic of Hershey's confectionery had Milton Hershey decided to look at other options!

Before we leave this chapter, this quote by Marcus Aurelius is a refreshing vibe that encourages one to reboot oneself and live life to the fullest whenever one wants.

> *"Your principles can't be extinguished unless you snuff out the thoughts that feed them, for it's continually in your power to reignite new ones. It's possible to start living again! See things anew as you once did—that is how to restart life!"*

CHAPTER 4

ANCIENT SHASTRAS TO BUSINESS SUTRAS: SIX LESSONS FOR ANCIPRENEURS

*I*n the 90s, everyone used to gather around the TV set to watch the telecast of Mahabharata and Ramayana, and every now and then, the elders in the family would point out teachings and moral values to wide-eyed kids. There used to be countless stories from scriptures and folktales that served as a legacy when grandparents would entertainingly narrate them to giggly kids during summer vacations. Well, today, when the world has turned digital and relationships have become virtual, it is the need of the hour to reflect on these same stories and bring them back to life with a different flavour!

> *"Business, as I have seen it, places one great demand on you: it needs you to self-impose a framework of ethics, values, fairness and objectivity on yourself at all times."*
>
> **– Ratan N Tata**

Shashtras, or Indian scriptures, are a rich repository of knowledge pertaining to several spheres, and this also includes some valuable lessons for modern-day entrepreneurs.[xlii, xliii, xliv, xlv, xlvi, xlvii, xlviii] Scriptures include the Vedas, treatises like Kautilya's *Arthashashtra*, *Manusmriti*, and *Viduraniti*, holy texts like *The Bhagwat Gita*, as well as epic mythologies.

In Sikhism, the teachings of Guru Nanak have a lot of lessons for entrepreneurs. For instance, in the prayer of Sikhs, the line *"Nanak Naam Chardi Kala, Tere Bhane Sarbat Da Bhala"* can be picked by entrepreneurs as a way of conducting business – to flourish together and not alone. The importance of social impact and the effects of profit-sharing on co-workers and team members cannot be undermined. An ancipreneur can take cues in simplicity, humility and sincerity of purpose from his sayings, which also teach how to face situations instead of running away.

When we look towards Jainism and Buddhism, we find core principles that could prove useful for entrepreneurs. The concept of Aparigraha in Jainism (non-attachment to possessions) encourages minimalism, and environmental consciousness is seen to have been adopted by clothing brands like Patagonia, who have a sustainable approach towards production and focus on minimising environmental impacts. Diversity of points of view and learning to see truth as several parts of a whole is the basis of 'Anekantavada', and in today's globalised business environment, it encourages leaders to consider multiple perspectives before making decisions.[xlix, l]

Parallels can be drawn between folklore in Buddhist scriptures that talk of mindful approaches and the principles of Satya Nadella at Microsoft, who often talks about the impact of developing self-awareness and mindfulness in a workflow. I think we all can agree on how meditative thinking makes us focused, even if practised for a few minutes each day!

The Buddhist EightFold paths can be incorporated into modern entrepreneurship practices like that of Right Speech aligns with transparent communication, Right Action with ethical business practices, and Right Livelihood with corporate responsibility.[li, lii, liii]

Both Jainism and Buddhism preach about the importance of compassion, which again is an important part of entrepreneurship—ensuring that one never loses the human touch while surviving in cut-throat competition.

Importance of 'gurus' - Mentorship counts!

> "*Akhandamandalaakaaram Vyaaptam yena Charaacharam*
>
> *Tatpadam Darshitam Yena Tasmaisri Gurave Namaha*"

We have been taught the importance of Gurus in our ancient texts. It is said that a Guru is someone who leads us from the darkness of ignorance into the shining light of wisdom.

In the Mahabharata, it is seen that Dronacharya, Bhisma and many other Acharyas, who are the common gurus of the royal princes, repeatedly dissuade Duryodhana from making rash decisions and injustice that would mar the reputation of the family. He disrespects them and overrules their advice, while the Pandavs, despite knowing that the Gurus would not be able to fight on their behalf, still come to them for invaluable advice and blessings.

Lord Rama could succeed in his war against Ravana due to the lessons learnt from his kul-guru (clan-guru) Vashisht as well as success mantras from Rishi Agastya. The lessons in 'Bala' and 'Atibala' given by Guru Vishwamitra ensured that Ram and Lakshman were not exhausted or sleepy during any situation during the exile as well as war. Ancient Greeks also had a tradition of Guru -Shishya tradition. So, Socrates was the mentor of Plato, Plato was the mentor of Aristotle, and Aristotle was the mentor of Alexander the Great. Now, you can imagine the importance of mentorship. It is said that even Mahatma Gandhi had a mentor, Gopal Krishna Gokhale, and similarly, Nelson Mandela had a mentor in Walter Sisulu.

Source: https://www.businessinsider.in/finance/bill-gates-reveals-why-warren-buffett-was-an-invaluable-source-of-support-during-the-stormiest-period-of-his-career/articleshow/69932313.cms

In the business world, we have seen some famous mentor-entrepreneur relationships bloom. Perhaps Microsoft, a budding venture of Bill Gates and Paul Allen, wouldn't have flourished had it not been for the expert guidance of benefactor Warren Buffet, who lent his advice on long-term strategies, overcoming tough situations as well as simplifying complex issues for Bill Gates, who was starting out in his entrepreneurial journey.

Oprah Winfrey, a popular talk show host and influencer, considers lessons in self-belief in taking action as well as learning to differentiate between friends and foes, from renowned American memoirist Maya Angelou, to be a turning point in her career.

Can you think of some more famous mentorship examples from business? Why not start making a list of your dream mentors from top companies right away?

Nepotism vs Talent

In the business world, an oft-made mistake is to trust partners and clients belonging to a reputed bloodline and going forward without really assessing the credibility of the person, simply on the basis of previous relationships with other members of the family. This nepotism (yeah, the term that has created much furore in Bollywood!) can be dangerous as the successor of wealth and companies may not necessarily be a worthy collaborator. In the business world, we see many examples of nepotism and the subsequent trial that follows. For instance, the US government is investigating the recruitment of children of Chinese officials by JP Morgan & Chase Co., which is thought to be a move for the growth of the business. Donald Trump's recruitment of his daughter, a model and a fashion designer, as his chief advisor raised quite a few eyebrows, and, in an interview, Ivanka Trump herself said that she wouldn't have made it this far if not for nepotism. In India also, we have various examples of politicians giving roles to their favourite person in Sports or Commerce, but we won't get into much as that is outside the scope of this book. However, the moot point is that nepotism in any form and in any field is bad. As business owners, we should always look for talent to grow our organisation.

This is something that the epic Mahabharata has several instances. Karna assumed to be the son of a low-born charioteer, is extremely talented but is time and again insulted and considered unworthy. He is refused a chance to showcase his skills at a weapons trial contest as the entire Hastinapur is eager to watch Arjuna's archery performance and is also rejected by Draupadi at the swayamvar, citing his lineage. One side's loss is another's gain, and Duryodhana recognises the diamond in the rough and wastes no time in befriending him- a move that benefits him in strategy planning and war tactics.

Consider the examples of Pandu, Dhritarashtra and Vidur. Pandu is cursed, Dhritarashtra is blind and morally unfit to be king, and that leaves Vidur—intellectually blessed, skilled and healthy. However, there's a catch! He's not the son of a queen but of a maid, and thereby, despite being better than the rest of his brothers, he is forced to remain in the shadow. Still, his tactics and planning help delay the destruction of Hastinapur's family, and he remains an important advisor. There is no doubt that had Vidur been chosen as king, the story of Mahabharata might have been different. The molestation, the murders, and the slaughters could have been prevented. A family and a kingdom could have been saved!

Another glaring example is that of Eklavya. Imagine a tribal boy gazing admiringly at the young princes receiving training and wishing that somehow his role model, Dronacharya, picks him to be his teacher. But alas! Upon approaching him, the young boy's request is turned down as Drona's entire focus is on training Arjuna, and he is bound by the rules of the state that forbid him from teaching anyone else apart from those belonging to the royal family. The young boy, son of the chief of the Nishada tribe of hunters, is stunned as he realises that just because he belongs to the Shudra caste, he is being rejected.

He does not give up and continues to train alone, keeping a statue of Dronacharya. It is hard work and years of practice that transforms him into such a skilful archer that he can shoot without looking, just by hearing the sound of the animal. One day, upon being irritated by the barking of the dog, he fires seven arrows in quick succession into the maw of the dog, and it runs off, unable to bark and is discovered by Dronacharya and Arjuna. They find Eklavya, and Arjuna's anger knows no bounds once he learns that he considers Drona to be his guru and is better than him. Realising the delicate nature of the situation, Drona asks him for his thumb as 'Guru-Dakshina' so that this talented archer is never a competitor for Arjuna again, and the devoted Eklavya accepts. Had nepotism not blinded the teacher-student duo, perhaps Eklavya could have been a useful ally in the Kurukshetra and would have been an apt answer to Karna's skill.

This really provokes us to think about who we are placing our trust in and choose who we want to work with as entrepreneurs, irrespective of caste, creed, religion, gender, inheritance and based purely on talent, hard work and skill. Successful companies now have anti-nepotism policies, and HR managers are trained to spot and stop these practices.

Strategic alliances for success

The ancient Indian scriptures always envision the world as a global family – *Vasudhaevakutumbakam*, and urge to shun individualistic desires in favour of *Sarvabhavantu Sukhinaha*. This approach has led many entrepreneurs to be extremely popular amongst their peers and clients.

In the Ramayana, an entrepreneur can find important lessons in alliances. Lord Rama and Lakshman were in exile, and to face the mighty army in Lanka, they needed a military alliance. They helped Sughriva gain back his kingdom and gained not only the loyal Vanar Sena but also his managerial skills. On the other hand, the arrogance and unjust actions of Ravana compelled his own brother to turn traitor to him and feed intel to his rival army. This is important.

Another instance of teamwork is when Lord Rama meditated upon how the mighty ocean would be crossed and finally found his answer in Nala and Nila, who had the gift of floatation on water. He sought the cooperation of local village folk, mobilised the Vanar Sena and prayed to the mighty river god for cooperation in building the stone bridge. He even appreciated the help of the little squirrels trying to help!

In the Mahabharata, strategic alliance building on and off the battlefield was a marvellous case in study. The alliances were made based on greed, familial connections, conscientious instincts, and revenge and were strong enough to sustain them till the end of the war.

Teamwork between Draupadi, Arjuna and Bheema helped lead evil molester Keechak to his death while they escaped in incognito mode. An ill-fated example of Chakravayu teamwork amongst the Kauravas led young Abhimanyu to a valiant death on the Kurukshetra battlefield—a reminder of what can happen if your enemies are slowly joining hands together to bring you down. A successful entrepreneur must go forth in business dealings not with half-baked knowledge like that of Abhimanyu with the Chakravyuh but with full information so as to avoid complex traps laid out for doom.

Businesses often team up with each other to tap into customer bases of each other. For example, when Apple Pay was about to be launched to enable contactless transactions for credit cards, the only credit card company that recognised the versatile technology and quickly partnered with Apple was Mastercard, so only iPhone users who had Mastercard had access to this benefit.

Targeting the luxury brands segment, Louis Vitton handbags were crafted to match the new BMW collections so as to lure specific female customers into their consumer base. Similarly, catering to the adrenaline-filled audiences of both companies, in 2012, RedBull and GoPro organised a skydiving event where RedBull sponsored the activity, and the skydiver could use a GoPro to record the experience.

Could you make a list of at least ten brands whose partnerships have worked in the last decade?

Business karma

> *"Karmanye Vadhikaraste Ma Phaleshu Kadachana Ma Karma Phala Hetur Bhurma tey Sangostva Akarmani"*
> **–The Bhagawat Gita**

This saying asks the individual to be responsible for the work that is to be done and fulfil it with sincerity of purpose without trying to control the outcomes or dwelling too much on the results. Inaction should not result from obsessing over the 'what-ifs.' This serves as an eye-opener for entrepreneurs who chase statistics, performance reports and profit trends rather than focussing on performance, continuous quality improvement and research. It also serves as a deterrent against overconfidence and

The concept of 'Karma', as explained by Lord Krishna, is based on the universal law of cause and effect, where anyone can write their own destiny through their deeds and thoughts. It also shows the way of detachment towards material pleasures, destruction of one's ego, and turning away from negative emotions that can drive one's focus away from the work at hand.

This has been echoed in the words of Mongolian conqueror Genghis Khan, "The mastery of pride, which was something more difficult, he explained, to subdue than a wild lion. If you can't swallow your pride, you can't lead."

Karma can form an important component of the ethical code of conduct in business and can be explained best with the following excerpt from Robert L. Heilbroner's book *The Worldly Philosophers*:

> "A man who permits his self-interest to run away with him will find that competitors have slipped in to take his trade away; if he charges too much for his wares or if he refuses to pay as much as everybody else for his workers, he will find himself without buyers in the one case and without employees in the other."

The keys to Wealth Management: Knowledge Acquisition, Financial Prudency, and Self Realisation

There are several lessons in financial management that the Vedas can impart to the ancipreneur. Contrary to popular belief, Indian scriptures do not just focus on sacrifice and detachment from the world but also lay out the roadmap as to how one can acquire and manage wealth resources. The Vedas instruct the individual to acquire as much wealth as possible without compromising on moral values and also to keep the influx of finances continuous by optimisation of multiple channels of income. It defines two types of financial resources: *Vittam* (wealth that is earned already) and *Vedyam* (wealth to be earned hereafter). It strongly emphasises the importance of being debt-free while devising capital structure and managing profits with fairness. Lessons from the Vedas have special sections devoted to relationship building through courteousness and kindness, succession management, equitable partnerships, multiculturalism, multi-linguism, quality control, and labour-fair practices.

Steve Jobs, founder of Apple, stresses the importance of listening to the inner voice: "*Your time is limited, so don't waste it living someone else's life. Don't be trapped by dogma – which is living with the results of other people's thinking. Don't let the noise of other's opinions drown out your own inner voice. And most important, have the courage to follow your heart and intuition. They somehow already know what you truly want to become. Everything else is secondary.*"

This is in tune with the 'Aham Brahmasmi' ('I am God') concept from Advaita philosophy as it seeks to unify the ideas of the Atman (self) with the Brahman or the Supreme Consciousness of the Universe. Meditation and self-introspection for entrepreneurs are highly advised so that they can achieve a good work-life balance. Techniques can range from Kriya Yoga to guided Vipassana, and these help in bringing back focus into lives.

Business operations must be carried out with knowledge acquisition and application. There are three principal concepts regarding the awareness of the individual – they must know the objects about which the information is to be gained (*Prameya*), the means by which the knowledge is acquired (*Pramana*) and lastly, an assessment of the self, and what capabilities or limitations exist for gaining the knowledge (*Pramata*).

> "*Yadeva vidyay¯ karoti praddhayopanijad¯ tadeva vŸryavattaram bhavati*"

This shloka demonstrates that whatever you may do, productivity and effectiveness increase when done with appropriate knowledge and faith.

Photograph by Getty Images as seen in https://www.outlookindia.com/magazine/story/dhirubhai-ambani-1932-2002-reliance/298633

This ancipreneurial lesson was probably known to Dhirubai Ambani, founder of Reliance Industries, whose rags-to-riches story is truly inspiring. Have you ever wondered how a simple Gujarati boy whose family had to borrow money from neighbours for basic sustenance and who once had to sell bhaji (fritters) could dream of something so big? But again, he strongly believed that being born poor is nobody's fault, but if one did not do anything to change this fact and died in the same financial state, then it was completely the individual's fault. His early beginnings were that of a clerk in Yemen, and still, his quest for knowing about different business processes was fuelled by his ambition.

> "Think big, think fast, think ahead. Ideas are no one's monopoly."
>
> **– Dhirubai Ambani**

At Besse and Co., where he worked as a clerk, he switched departments so that he could learn different aspects of financial management, commodity trading, purchase and sales, and record-keeping. He even went to drink tea at expensive restaurants so that he could learn from the conversations of wealthy businessmen. He worked for free at a Gujarati trading firm to learn about speculative trading and read books ranging from history to psychology. Throughout the expansion phase of Reliance Industries, this know-how greatly helped him make smart business choices.

The next case study in wealth management is that of J. D Rockefeller of Standard Oil. Rockefeller was a strategic mastermind, creating a trillion-dollar business with money-saving tactics. One of these tactics was vertical integration—eliminating middlemen and saving on costs. For example, instead of buying barrels for oil storage and transportation, he supplied his own timber and made his own! By owning the whole supply chain, Standard Oil could decrease oil prices significantly. Not only did this save them money, but it allowed them increased production power, which led them on the path towards market domination.

Rockefeller was a financial mastermind who kept track of every penny he earned and spent in a detailed ledger. This man was no spendthrift despite having an impressive net worth. He chose to live modestly, preferring to invest his money back into Standard Oil. In fact, he would buy additional shares whenever possible, proving his unshakable faith in the company's success. Whenever he did splash out on something, you can bet that it was intentional and well thought out!

Having a proficient accountant on your team is vital for running a successful business. It is recommended to have regular meetings with them to discuss financial changes, make informed business decisions, and identify potential cost-cutting opportunities. Rockefeller climbed to the top of the wealth ladder by reducing waste and inefficiencies. Mimic his brilliance by searching for money leaks in your business's expenses during meetings with your accountant. Eliminating pointless costs is also an option, but aim for those that positively affect your bottom line!

Insights for ancipreneurs:

- Mentorship is necessary for sustaining momentum in your business endeavours as the experiences and skills instilled are accurately suited to the problems.
- Favour talent and hard work as criteria for choosing employees and partners. Avoid nepotism at all costs.
- Build strategic connections with ally companies with similar audience demographics and behavioural traits to have a win-win situation in terms of potential leads.
- Do not try to sabotage your rivals, as it affects your credibility in the long run. Also, take steps to protect yourself from attacks, whether in the virtual or the physical space.
- Keep acquiring knowledge for generating new streams of income, wealth management as well as prudent investments.
- Check invoices for contract work, maintenance fees, shipping expenses, and other regular costs to discover where you're losing money. Start making a plan to cut down on these expenses, like hiring a web developer who won't break the bank but will fix things at a moment's notice. Regular cost-cutting measures

and investments, where necessary, will help you stay afloat for a longer time.

Activity 1: One of the most successful organisations in India identifies with the following five core values:

1) Integrity

We will be fair, honest, transparent and ethical in our conduct; everything we do must stand the test of public scrutiny.

2) Responsibility

We will integrate environmental and social principles into our businesses, ensuring that what comes from the people goes back to the people many times over.

3) Excellence

We will be passionate about achieving the highest standards of quality, always promoting meritocracy.

4) Pioneering

We will be bold and agile, courageously taking on challenges using deep customer insight to develop innovative solutions.

5) Unity

We will invest in our people and partners, enable continuous learning, and build caring and collaborative relationships based on trust and mutual respect.

Which of the takeaways from this chapter on Indian scriptures can you find in the vision and mission statement of this organisation?

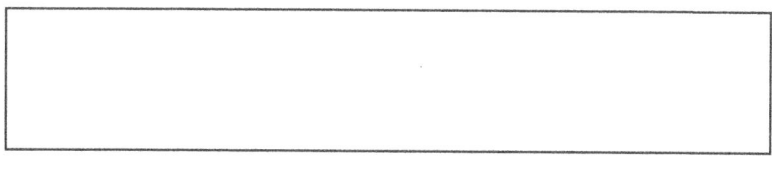

 *Trivia – This vision and mission statement has been procured from the official website of the Tata Group of Institutions (with business verticals of steel, automobile, retail, telecom, media, trading, investments, technology, aerospace and defence) is a brilliant example of how vision with ethics can transform a venture into a booming success in the competitive landscape.*

Tata is known for following a strict code of conduct by which all associates and employees abide. It has demonstrated the power of effective leadership with strong values with its philanthropic activities and ambitious but people-centric approach over the years.

Activity: You are a media mogul and own a multi-million-dollar company. You give all key positions to your sons and other family members. Your son is unworthy and is embroiled in controversies. Despite protests from employees and criticism, you do not stop your nepotism. You are finally sued for it in court after you purchased your daughter's media company. What could you have done differently to support your family's dreams and yet not compromise on the company's needs?

Trivia: Since July 2011, Rupert Murdoch and his company, the News Corporation, have come under intense scrutiny for wrongdoings. Subsequently, he had to face a lawsuit filed by the Amalgamated Bank of New York and the Central Laborers Pension Fund, who accused him of nepotism and the company of paying for his daughter's media firm as well as financial transactions of family members. He was termed in a book as the worst media mogul, as the erosion of the stakeholders' trust and investments was unpardonable.

Activity: Imagine yourself from a small Ukranian village, born to a struggling family without resources. When you were young, your family shifted to California, and you had to support them in making ends meet. You loved computers and started to read whenever you had time, and by the time you were eighteen, you were equipped with computing skills that would eventually land you a job at Yahoo! as an infrastructure engineer. But there is so much competition, and you don't have any backing or financial resources to stand out amidst thousands of other employees. How would you make use of your talent to do something unique?

> Space for readers to write

Trivia: Well, Jan Koum is the person in this little anecdote. After ten years of serving in Yahoo! he founded WhatsApp and transformed communication in the virtual world. He couldn't rely on any family inheritance or influence to rise in the ranks of his job, so he used his skill sets and experience to create a wave in the social media setup.

Never underestimate what a talent honed out of hard work and perseverance can achieve!

Activity: You are a book enthusiast who needs to get through with some clothes shopping for the day but is looking to relax during this experience with a caffeine-filled experience. Do you know of two brands that teamed up with a leading coffee-serving brand for customers like you?

CHAPTER 5

ANCIPRENEUR LESSONS FROM HEBRAISM, CHRISTIANITY, AND ISLAM

*H*ebrew and Christian texts are deeply ingrained in short parables, quotes, and morals that give insights into the basic fabric of the human psyche and have influenced many entrepreneurs over the course of time.[liv] We all know the story of the Good Samaritan that our grandparents used to quote when explaining the importance of compassion. Similarly, there are many Christian virtues that can help ancipreneurs hold on to morality in business.

Islamic religious texts, including the Quran and Hadith (sayings of the Prophet Muhammad), are replete with interesting anecdotes that offer valuable business lessons.

Let us examine some examples from the scriptures of these religions that can help pave the correct path for modern-day entrepreneurs.

Why Stewardship is Important?

In this concept given by the parable of the talents (Matthew 25:14–30), resources like time, talent, energy, natural sources, money, etc., are entrusted to us as if we are stewards of this gift, and their responsible utilisation is a virtue everyone must practice. We see many brands reflecting this kind of ethos.

Businesses like IKEA adopt sustainable practices in their production line, choosing to use environmentally friendly materials and responsible energy usage to minimise greenhouse gas emissions and cut down on harmful waste products. They are consciously switching to responsible natural sourcing of raw materials, and this is seen in the way they have switched from fossil-based glues to bio-based glues. Similarly, they have tied up with solar energy parks so that their carbon footprint is reduced. Their campaigns often have phrases like becoming "climate positive" and commitment to "global stewardship" and "forest stewardship" which is also seen in their afforestation drives in an effort to compensate for their sourcing from the forests. This kind of sustainable business practice can attract loyal customers from across the globe who want to associate with brands who are serious about saving the planet!

Diligence is always rewarded

In the Hebrew Book of Proverbs, we can find a quote from King Solomon (Proverbs 6:6), where he says, *"Go to the ant, you sluggard; consider its ways and be wise!"* Here, the ant is considered to be a symbol of tenacity and preparedness for the future, and he says in several places later about the laziness of people, imploring them to wake up and take charge of their destiny. This sentiment also finds a place in New Testaments (Thessalonians 5:14), where God warns against those who are lazy and urges them to earn the food that they eat.

Business is all about action-taking, and a lazy entrepreneur who falls into complacency can never flourish. Every day is about trying new techniques, maintaining standards and taking care of the entire machinery that has to run like clockwork else disaster can be imminent.

The Golden Rule

According to the Golden Rule in Christianity: "Do unto others as you would have them do unto you" (Matthew 7:12), the principle of treating everyone with the same courtesy and kindness that one expects out of others is advocated.

Ancipreneurs could tailor their customer service policies and frameworks to be more proactive in helping customers address their concerns and to adopt compassion and empathy while dealing with customers. This has been embodied in the approach of Southwest Airlines Co., which treats its customers with respect on a priority basis and is known for its top-notch customer service program.

Similarly, this approach is also necessary for developing coordination among the team members working on a project where the spirit of togetherness is given precedence over hierarchy.

Where Every Individual Counts

The story in The Parable of the Lost Sheep (Luke 15:3-7) tells us about a shepherd who loses one of his sheep out of his flock of a hundred and then goes to search for it. This teaches about the importance of every individual in the team. In a world where culling of job positions and new acquisitions are increasingly becoming common, an employee-focused approach can prove to be beneficial for fostering loyal connections within the company that can strengthen it from within.

This can be seen in the Starbucks coffee company, which has a strong employee welfare program focussing on tuition fees for their children, stock options, etc. This should be emulated by ancipreneurs for recognising and rewarding every employee who may tend to feel undervalued sometimes in a corporate set-up. Happier employees lead to strong companies; it's simple!

The story of the Widow's Mite (Mark 12:41-44), where a poor widow's small offering is considered great because of her sacrifice, again tells us about this kind of approach where an employee's smallest contribution must be recognised. Similarly, the act of Jesus' act of washing his disciples' feet (John 13:1-17) teaches about leading while serving others and could serve as a models for internal leadership within companies where employees are also regarded as significant driving forces and stakeholders.

You know, when you really think about it, the stories and teachings from Christianity have a lot to offer the business world. They bring to the forefront values like showing respect, genuinely caring for each individual, being generous, encouraging innovation, and practicing servant leadership.

Many unique stories in Islam also teach us about the ethical way of doing business. The stories offer a different perspective that calls for deeper introspection in ancipreneurs.[lv, lvi]

Zakat and Philanthropy in the Corporate World

Zakat is a way of giving back to the community in the form of not just charity but as a system of wealth circulation. After an Islamic individual reaches a certain threshold (known as *nisab*), they can participate in almsgiving and donate 1/40th or 2.5% of their wealth. This is considered nearly as pious as praying in Islam.

The corporate analogue of Zakat has been seen in the SalesForce company, whose founder, Marc Benioff, visualised the two pillars of philanthropy and profitability, establishing the reputed 1-1-1 model. This model pledges 1% of each of the equity of the company, products and employee time back to the community. Every year, they participate in donation drives and voluntarism in needy communities and have already made a significant change in global healthcare. This pledge, the 1% model, has also been adopted by more than 8500 companies across the world.

Collaborative Decision Making: The Principle of Shura

Leadership in Islam is not just about giving commands but about consultative decision-making. The doctrine of *Shura* in the Quranic verses talks about taking consultation in conducting affairs, and this can be translated in business as the culture of participative management.[lvii, lviii] In the Islamic texts, Caliph Umar Ibn Al-Khattab was known for his consultative style. Organisations are regularly judged on their quality standards based on several criteria, one of which is participative management, i.e. how employees, stakeholders, and business heads can collaborate for collective business decisions. This ensures the maintenance of inclusivity and a sense of community benefit necessary for the removal of bias, the dawning of fresh perspectives, as well as nurturing of company loyalists. For example, Google as a company is extremely focussed on a collaborative employee interaction framework where all voices are heard and feedback is generated for analysis and corrective measures.

Morally upright Islamic framework for ancipreneurs

The concepts of *khayr* (goodness), *birr* (righteousness), *qist* (equity), *'adl* (equilibrium and justice) from the Quran have to be assimilated by the ancipreneur while carrying out business dealings. There are several anecdotes that talk of the honesty of Prophet Muhammed in business dealings. Before his time as the prophet, he worked as a merchant at Mecca, and upon being informed about a defect in the sold item, he promptly offered a full refund. In fact, his business partnership and later marriage with Khadijah bint Khuwaylid, a successful businesswoman, was based on his honesty and sharp business sense, which she could know about after she hired him for a trading expedition to Syria and then on subsequent business trips.

There are several sayings in the Islamic scriptures that point ancipreneurs towards morally sound business practices. For instance, there's a Hadith where the Prophet Muhammad said, "Pay the worker his wages before his sweat dries." This talks about fair and timely wages as well as employee welfare. Even the concepts of risk (Mudarabah)and profit sharing in Islamic finance systems help in ethical business practices. For example, Dubai Islamic Bank follows a profit-sharing service-based system and is well renowned for its ethical dealings.

A sense of universal brotherhood prevails in Islamic business dealings owing to the principle of *Ukhuwah* where the businessman is supposed to treat his fellowmen in the same way that he expects himself to be treated, and there are doctrines that teach us that cheating anyone is *haram* (prohibited), whether Muslim or non-Muslim.

Islamic business practices are ingrained with strong ethics with an iron-clad will to fulfil the duties of the supreme power. Ancipreneurs need to adopt this resilient and strong-willed approach while developing their moral compass in business dealings.

Key Insights for Ancipreneurs

- The importance of transparency and honesty in business dealings cannot be undervalued as these lead to trust-building amongst customers as well as can pave the way for strategic partnerships.
- Corporate philanthropy is an important aspect of any business, and ancipreneurs should choose areas of society to make an impact through their products/services, financial as well as manpower resources.
- Every individual voice counts and should be taken into account in terms of decision-making, welfare practices or formulating strategies for the future.
- Sustainable practices need to be adopted within the company's framework so as to fulfil the social responsibility of effective stewardship of resources.

Activity 1: As an ancipreneur, make a list of areas where you could fulfil your Pledge 1% initiative. You could also try choosing impact fields that resonate with your business and would align with the philanthropic ideas of your company in a better way.

Activity 2: What committees can you constitute within your company to promote decentralisation and participative management? What are the mechanisms that you would adopt to ensure a collaborative decision-making process in your company?

CHAPTER 6

TALES FROM THE MEDITERRANEAN DEPTHS TO THE PYRAMIDAL PEAKS

Networking with ingenuity

In ancient times, Phoenicia was an influential area that dispatched expert engineers, craftsmen and skilled **sailors** to establish a network by barter of services, ideas and goods, and this impacted the cultural and communicative development in the Mediterranean basin. About 750-650 BC, which is thought to be the Archaic period of Greece, saw the peak of Phoenician seafaring and merchant activities that ultimately influenced what we know as classical Greece.

With their exuberant trading affairs, the early Canaanites established the first beginnings of Multinational Enterprises with dealings in diverse goods like silver, ivory, textiles, tin, copper, iron and locally manufactured goods from the Mediterranean that took place in widely spaced geographical locations like Spain, Britain, Africa, Cyprus, and Syria, There are a lot of texts that marvel at how these tribesmen could manage intercontinental trade uniting Africa, Europe, and Asia Minor. The pieces of evidence from Ugaritic and Ras Shamra texts show transnational partnerships and the rise of militarisation of the Phoenician commerce system to counteract threats during seafaring. Protection of goods and sailing merchants began to be recognised in treatises.

Quoting Richard Harrison, a renowned British archaeologist:

> *"The pattern of Phoenician trade was linked to specialist production centres, connecting different areas and political systems which otherwise would not have been drawn together, and establishing a rate of exchange much to their own advantage. They could do this fairly easily since they had a monopoly on both the specialised manufactures that everyone desired, and the marine transport, so they could stimulate demand where they chose to do so. A virgin market was the ideal since it could be scoured hard for huge profits; this accounts for their interest in Spain, especially in the silver mines behind Huelva in the Rio Tinto, and near Castulo in the Sierra Morena. The Phoenicians were able to locate new metal sources, and unlock the wealth from them, unhindered, for a century and a half. The traders worked through a system of Phoenician family firms, who had representatives in their home town in the eastern Mediterranean as well as in their new markets and factories; they owned their own ships, too, and were*

prepared to take risks which their overlords could not well calculate, or were unwilling to do, and so profited greatly."

Source: Illustration by Robert Clifford Magis, National Geographic

Anthropologist Ralph Linton says in his publication *Tree of Culture* that what set apart the Phoenician entrepreneurs is their zeal for networking and profit-making rather than the plundering

Source: These depictions of Phoenician ships come from the palace of Assyrian King Sargon II. (Wikimedia)

policies of the Babylonians and Assyrians. A collection of essays about these activities has been made into a book titled *'La civilisation phenicienne et punique: Manuel de recherché.'*

As for agricultural advancements, the Phoenicians introduced crop specialisation, technologies, commercial farming practices (surplus cereals) and olive oil production. Commerce also introduced banqueting and transport amphorae, along with standardised weights, measures, and seals. Aside from Mesopotamian astronomy, Phoenician merchants brought their own alphabet: a phonetic system that used words, not pictographs. In addition to promoting urban growth, the city's artisans, merchants, and agents invested in major capital projects and promoted literacy. Mercantile networks were also successful because of industry. In this period, long-distance trade and exchange took place in a peaceful manner. It is believed that flasks and beads, such as the ones made in Spain, were transported by the thousands across the Mediterranean. In Spain, wheel-turned pottery was also introduced and mass-produced. Phoenician's ingenuity can be demonstrated by the example of how one of Sicily's sparsely populated islands was turned into a thriving wine-making and trading centre thanks to its efforts. It is suggested that knowledge of the tidal activity, currents, coastal topography, and Mediterranean winds greatly helped Phoenician traders to determine suitable speeds, routes and timings of their journeys and trading activities.

In the book *Negotiate Like the Phoenicians*, the principles that the Phoenicians adhered to are cultural sensitivity, ingenuity, adventurous spirit, fair play, and clear communication. The author, Habib Chamoun-Nicolas, explains how buyer-seller alliances, win-win situations, and step-by-step networks allowed Phoenicians to stay afloat while neighbouring civilisations fell into a deep ensuing 'Dark Age.'

The exploits of the Canaanites and Phoenicians emphasised the importance of the travel economy. The merchants hailing from these places were sophisticated and literate, with preferences towards luxury goods. The impressive contribution of Phoenician city-states to advancing urban civilisation and sparking an influx of technological innovation has been well documented. Reflecting the systematised way trade was managed and controlled and bolstered by strong religious and feudal connections, the impact of Phoenician city-states can still be seen in modern societies.

Like the Phoenicians expanded their trade networks through cultural communications, trade alliances, merchant connections, and technological barter, networking in business is crucial as it allows other people and businesses to become aware of your presence and contributes to the establishment of relationships. Reputation is also increased through regular participation in networks. Benchmarking allows you to compare your business with similar organisations, highlighting areas of strength and potential for improvement. Business networks are the perfect place to find out what's new, such as must-know legal requirements or cutting-edge tech as well as for identifying new customers and suppliers, either from within the group or through established recommendations.

Engaging in networking activities is a valuable pursuit that provides wider opportunities to gain information and skills and potentially establish partnerships. Strategically aligning with the appropriate individuals, particularly marketers who share an active interest in collaborating with you, can significantly enhance your chances of success.

Let me give you an example here. Despite being an international scientific and trade conference, the Paris Electrical Exhibition of 1881 provided Thomas Edison with an opportunity to expand his contacts and assess his competitors due to the presence of his team.

E-commerce giants like Etsy and eBay skyrocketed in popularity by embracing the network effect and opening up possibilities for consumers to access their products - while ridesharing services rose up the ranks with the same strategy! Uber and Lyft rode the wave of success thanks to their expanding population of users across cities and states! As the Uber and Lyft fleets swelled, so too did their market value!

Walmart's exemplary logistics offer unparalleled convenience to customers, making it effortless to have what they need right at their fingertips. Walmart is setting the bar with their forward-thinking supply chain management and expansive product range, allowing them to make sweeping changes like transitioning to renewable energy and re-imagining its packaging - all while keeping costs low. The company soared to success thanks to the revolutionary internal value network transformation!

facebook Facebook is an exemplary illustration of a social media company with a direct value network! With Facebook, you'll be part of a massive worldwide value network—and connecting with it is only a click away!

Facebook creates a world of connection with Messenger, live streaming, traditional posts, curated groups and suggested content, all tailored to each user's interests. With Facebook, you can connect your business to the world, reach out to customers with targeted ads, create a compelling business page and tap into a powerful network that opens up valuable leads.

Ancient African Tactics: Lessons in Innovation & Diplomacy

Sketch of King Shaka (1781 - 1828) from 1824
Ssource: Wikimedia Commons

The ancient African rulers and tribe leaders had a unique sense of leadership and never lost sight of the goal at any cost. Shaka Zulu was renowned for his military prowess and his vision of innovation and adaptability for the expansion of the Zulu kingdom with new combat techniques and diverse weapons. The leadership qualities of Shaka Zulu are still respected today owing to his drive for discipline, continuous improvement upon his rivals through collection and analysis of enemy troop positions and strategies, adaptability to a variety of conditions, efficient resource management, and tuning his warriors to act swiftly while also planning for long-term impacts.

His renowned 'bull-horn' war formation strategy can be a lesson for entrepreneurs of today, and we draw parallels here between this military tactic and what it can mean for business owners.[lix, lx]

Table: The Bull-Horn Technique in War and Business

Components	In War	Impacts	Application In Business
The Head	• Central part of formation • Experienced warriors • Engage directly with enemy	Intense weakening of rivals by head-on battle	Strengthening the core product/service (the head) and giving importance to pioneers in the company.
The Horns	• Flanking the formation • Younger, faster warriors • Attack suddenly in pincer movement, circling around in surprise attack	Element of surprise and panic	Encircling the market by addressing multiple customer segments simultaneously (the horns) with quick innovations.

The Loins	<ul><li>Positioned behind head</li><li>Reserve forces</li><li>Pursue fleeing enemies or reinforce formation</li></ul>	Flexibility and adaptability to recover from any situation. It's what we call 'leaving no stones unturned'	Resource allocation and diversification of roles

This kind of vision has also been seen in many African tribes like the Masai and Yorubu tribes. Brands like Nike never fail to surprise their competitors with their innovative designs and trendy marketing, and we can definitely use this as an example of how the Zulu war tactics can be incorporated into the business.

Source: UNESCO series on women in African history, GLAM-WIKI partnership. Wikimedia Commons

While engaging with enemies is important, an equally significant component of business is diplomacy, something that Queen Nzinga was exceptionally good at. Although she suffered setbacks in the form of defeats and betrayals, it was her excellent negotiation skills and inclusive approach that helped her forge alliances. When faced with Portuguese enemy forces, she adopted Christianity to engage more effectively with the Portuguese officers while also maintaining her African culture and governance, secretly forming alliances with different African states and the Dutch forces, who were sworn enemies of the Portuguese.

Her leadership style was based on an intelligent, participatory mechanism where she marched into battle with her soldiers while also instructing them as to when to fiercely launch into combats and when to lie low as she negotiated terms with the enemies, saving lives and resources.

This kind of intelligence in business helps in forming strategic partnerships even with competitors, like that in the case of Apple and Samsung collaborating for smartphone components even while competing with each other. We can also take the example of Amazon, which competes fiercely in certain markets while, in some, it prefers to collaborate to sustain its business amongst the dominant market forces.

Queen Nzinga's legacy offers timeless lessons in leadership, strategy, resilience, cultural intelligence, and the balance between conflict and cooperation.

Determination in the dignity of labour

In the story of Djekhy & Son, funeral service providers around the temples of Egypt, the German Egyptologist August Eisenlohr, in the year 1885, chanced upon some papyri that painted a vivid picture of their dealings over the years.

Djekhy and his child Iturech were funeral priests who were paid to offer items to the deceased. In present-day language, we would refer to them as memorial service providers. By using the Greek description of their profession, they are referred to as choachytes, water-bearers. For some form of reward, they would deliver offerings to the mummies in the Theban graveyard, possibly once every week, on holy days, on the birthdays of the perished, and maybe even on their demise anniversaries. The archive tells us that Djekhy and Iturech not only provided funeral offerings but also had a great inclination towards farming. Multiple times, we discover Djekhy partnered with business associates leasing large flax fields. His son, Iturech, leased out fields that had been given to him as payment for his services to the deceased in the Theban necropolis. It appears that he had expanded their family business, transitioning from tenant to proprietor in a short span of time.

Tsenhor is considered one of the most prominent Egyptian woman entrepreneurs and was much like Djekhy and Iturech—a choachyte or funeral service provider given the duty of bringing offerings to those buried in the west bank necropolis of the Nile. Supposedly, she and her husband Psenese had been together for around five years and - if our guess is accurate—Tsenhor had become Psenese's business associate in some of his construction efforts by that point and since she was nearing her fortieth year then. She managed her business while running her family and stayed independent throughout her life.

In modern society also, we find people who are doing menial jobs. As ancipreneurs, we need to give respect to any job or profession and should never look down upon anyone. This is a valuable lesson we should always remember in our life.

Avoid obsessive radicalism in your approach

Pharaoh Amenhotep IV took his father's devotion to Aten to great heights. Soon after he came into reign, he changed his name to Akhenaten—Living Soul of Aten—and restricted himself to being the only communicator between the real world and Aten. That action rendered the priesthood of Amen-Re dormant. Yet even that was not enough for Akhenaten; he ordered the name of the past deity be eliminated from all formal buildings as well as writings, with certain instances of his father's pharaonic title demolished because it began with 'Amen.'

Ultimately, Akhenaten decreed a new capital be built and given over exclusively to worshipping Aten, thereby satisfactorily breaking away from traditions. He established Amarna—located 200 miles north of Thebes—and the focal point there was an immense hall dedicated to Aten. Unfortunately, in year 12 of Akhenaten's rule, in which a large gathering honouring Aten happened, Queen Nefertiti passed away; some experts believe Akhenaten himself had assigned her various administrative responsibilities. His mother, Queen Tiye, alongside one of his daughters, perished soon afterwards too; these fatalities immensely harmed Akhenaten, which caused him to intensify his fidelity toward Aten and strive harder against other Egyptian gods. However, Amenhotep IV did not manage to fulfil his endeavours since he himself died mysteriously in 1336 B.C.E., according to historians. With that,

Akhenaten's reverence for Aten terminated with him; shortly after his death, citizens ran back to Thebes, where they reverted back to their ancient religious observances and habits. Furthermore, due to Akhenaten's extreme passion for eradicating former faith, he neglected many other matters, including as portrayed by the newly discovered "Amarna Letters," in which monarchs and dignitaries are requesting Egypt for assistance on different issues of intruder attacks.

Firestone

It is important for entrepreneurs to discard old beliefs and welcome change rather than radically attempting to change things overnight. These often lead to wrong decisions, as in the case of the Firestone brand. A company that was synonymous with strength, success and company values suddenly found itself in deep trouble with the advent of radial tyres. The CEO invested over $400 million in radial tyre plant setups but clung to obsolete ways of production. Firestone officials refused to close down bias tyre plants despite inefficiencies, inferior quality and product recalls. As a result, it faced the loss of shares, bid for a takeover, and finally was acquired by Bridgestone. The Nokia phone is another example from which we can draw some lessons. Once upon a time, Nokia was a market leader in Indian markets. However, it never adapted to the changing times when smartphones and new technology emerged. Slowly, it was wiped out from the market as other brands took the leadership position, and Nokia became history. The same thing happened with car brands like Ambassador and Premier Padmini, which did not adapt themselves and lost to other foreign car companies in the Indian market.

Leading by example for a long and prosperous stint

The prominent Ramses II, also known as Ramses the Great, was the third pharaoh of the 19th dynasty in Egypt and is remembered in history as one of the most courageous and prudent military leaders. During his rule, Egypt witnessed remarkable feats of warfare and massive growth in its territorial boundaries. At an early age, Ramses joined his father on expeditions to war, and by 22 years old, he was heading the Egyptian military. It is noteworthy that as a young pharaoh, Ramses II contested hard-fought battles to guard Egypt's boundaries against the Hittites, Nubians, Libyans, and Syrians.

Cairo Museum display of Ramses II capturing his enemies (1250 BC), as sourced from Wikipedia

The Sherden sea pirates were a major danger to sailors trading on behalf of ancient Egyptians, who found themselves at dire risk due to the fear instilled by these buccaneers. To put an end to this threat, Ramses laid out a tactical strategy with remarkable boldness that extinguished the burning reign of terror practised by the Sherden Sea Pirates, attaining deep reverence for this accomplishment and garnering further admiration among those in his court.

Ramses II had a great love for architecture. During his extended reign, he constructed and reconstructed many structures, monuments, and temples. During his rule, there were many magnificent architectural works of diverse layouts and designs. Ramses II had a major fascination with architecture. During his long rule, he built and reconstructed several structures, monuments, and temples. His reign saw great architectural achievements in terms of diversity and design.

Being the third pharaoh of ancient Egypt, he is credited as one of the world's earliest rulers to sign a peaceful treaty. The battle of Kadesh did not reach its end result, so both sides decided to adhere to a peace agreement. What the particulars entailed remains obscure, but it is assumed that the Hittites avoided Egyptian soil and respected the accord.

This is a message for ancipreneurs to set examples by taking the initiative themselves and not hide behind the accomplishments of their predecessors or repeat their mistakes. Ramses-II not only culturally elevated the region and brought peace by skilfully leading the war campaigns, he also reduced the prevalent chaos, thus influencing many of his followers. Similarly, team members can only respect a leader who brings prosperous tidings by taking action himself and not merely issuing commands aggressively.

Insights for ancipreneurs:

- Need a solution to your business struggles? Reach out to your network and get advice from people who have been in your shoes before. Find the best way to push through your problem! Networking with other businesses can be your shortcut to streamlined operations, so don't forget to leverage the best practice guidance on offer! Connect and see where it leads! You may just find the perfect business opportunity or partner in your networking efforts!

There are no small or insignificant ventures. If you find a niche that no one else is willing to venture into, you should start brainstorming ideas on how to transform the opportunity into long-term business plans. There is dignity in every kind of venture, and those who recognise this can succeed as pioneers!

- One should know when to engage in competition and when to form strategic alliances with competitors. The power of negotiation is invaluable in business.
- Always take your rivals by surprise with quick, innovative tactics while maintaining your core strength and effectively deploying different resources and skilled manpower for diverse arenas.
- Blind investments without nullifying rigidity in product line development, as well as processes, can cost you heavily. Spend time and money on upgrades.
- Solving problems with deep commitment and leading by example ensures the longevity of the business as not only is an entrepreneur aware of all risks and challenges but also has the opportunity to show to the board members, employees and consumers that he/she is fully equipped to deal with any situation.

Activity 1:

Step 1: Make a list of all the networking events in your domain that you can attend this year. Note whether they are in physical, virtual, or hybrid mode.

Step 2: Find out which partners, suppliers, and rivals are going to attend it.

Step 3: Identify the pressing problems of your company. Are you looking for fresh recruits? Solutions from conference talks by speakers?

Step 4: Position delegates from your team to attend the networking events.

Step 5: Organise a pre- and post-event meeting to gain insights on actionable items.

Activity 2: Make a table like this for your competitors and figure out various aspects of collaboration and competition with them. Make use of your lessons from ancient Africa.

Competitor	Core Strength	Weaknesses	Current Strategy	Competitors (Place a Tick wherever it is possible to collaborate with their rival)	Possible Alliance In the Area of

CHAPTER 7

THE LEARNED LATIN-AMERICANS OF YORE

$\mathcal{B}$efore the Spanish invasion in the 1500s, three ancient civilisations—the Aztecs, Mayans, and the Incas—thrived in the southern American region. They were renowned for their distinct culture and sophisticated ways of trade, agriculture, and technology.

Let us explore the learnings from these three cultures that can help us transform into better ancipreneurs.[lxi, lxii]

Sustainable Resource Utilisation

It is surprising to see how all three civilisations came up with innovations in agriculture that could cater to the needs of their people but in harmony with nature. They adopted practices that were sustainable, economical, as well as effective utilisation of available resources.

The Incas were experts in managing the production of crops with effective management of resources. On the one hand, they practised terrace farming to conserve water and prevent soil erosion and on the other, they used crop rotation to preserve soil fertility. Similarly, the Mayans used slash-and-burn agriculture instead of cutting down entire forests for their sustenance, which led to the conservation of valuable forest cover that provided them with food and medicines.

This kind of responsible resource utilisation is also seen in clothing brands like Patagonia, which are committed to sustainable practices in their production line, minimising the environmental impact. They use organically grown material in their clothing line, and about 87% of Patagonia products are produced from recycled material. Their commitment towards reducing dependency on fossil fuels and the emission of gases and wastewater is truly remarkable.

The unique agricultural innovation that the Aztecs came up with was that of floating chinampas—a concept that maximised crop production while making the most out of the landscapes available.

AEROFARMS This approach has been adopted by the AeroFarms company, which has patented aeroponics technology, making their award-winning vertical farming approaches possible. This makes agriculture accessible with minimal waste, as they reduce the wastage of water by 95% and use no pesticides, herbicides or fungicides. Their indoor farming techniques involve speed breeding in batches with a sophisticated lighting system that ensures year-round growing of micro-crops.

Ancipreneurs should come up with innovative practices that could sustain themselves as well as others in the long run by figuring out how to maximise efficiency and resource utilisation while minimising wastage and negative impacts on their environment.

Centralised Planning and Trade Networks

Aztecs specialised in centralised planning, particularly in the cities of Texcoco, Tlacopan and Tenochtitlan (which later became capital), and the economic dynamics between the nobles and commoners were complex but well-planned. Their large and prosperous empire could be overseen effectively by their competent management. Also, their bustling marketplaces are seen as epitomes of resourceful organisation, a trait that can be seen in online marketplaces like Alibaba and Amazon. We also can take the example of Walmart, where the supply chain system and centralised distribution networks are reminiscent of the Aztec kind of management.

Maya Mask (250-600 AD) from National Museum of Anthropology in Mexico City, image sourced from Wikipedia.

The extensive trade networks established by the Mayans were based on both daily requirement items like food, clothing, tools, salt and fish as well as 'prestige items' like precious metals, artwork, crafts, and obsidian. Maritime trade networks were established through different types of vessels like canoes and rafts going to and forth a number of designated ports like El Meco, Chac

Balam, Cerros, and Jaina, among many others. It is interesting to note that the market system of the Mayas was highly regulated, with royals as well as merchants participating in the buying and selling of commodities.

An important factor in the establishment of effective communication and trading across challenging terrains was the incredible engineering skills of the Incas, which led to efficient transport systems via the Inca Road Network, which was also known as *Qhapaq Ñan* (royal road), connecting 40,000 km of territory. Meticulous planning with warehouses and restrooms dotting the network proved to be important in the transport of goods and the movement of traders. This kind of efficient management of logistics is seen in FedEx, which covers large routes for the transport of goods.

Looking Beyond the Mundane

What sets any Ancipreneur apart is the sense of creating something unique that can be a legacy product. The Mayans were far ahead of their time in innovations. They realised the importance of creating lifestyle products curated for those who could afford luxury items or had an aesthetic sense. These were actively used in barter for essential commodities, as well as participated in cultural exchanges from different regions, which is why the Mayan artisans were so valued. We see this kind of recognition for unique aesthetic items in the online marketplace Etsy, Kickstarter, and Montblanc, where small businesses easily sell many such exclusive handicrafts.

Similarly, their astrological charts, celestial predictions and mathematical contributions were a legacy that was painstakingly carved for future generations and made the entire civilisation more advanced and well-prepared. Today, we can think of Elon Musk's SpaceX program as an example of such technological innovation that could benefit future generations.

The Aztec, Mayan, and Inca civilisations are indeed examples of how principles such as sustainable resource management, the value of trade networks, organisational efficiency, reciprocity, and skilled craftsmanship have timeless relevance.

Key Insights for Ancipreneurs

- Focus towards sustainability is key to success, and thereby, minimising waste while maximising resource utilisation is an important skill for ancipreneurs.
- The logistical networks of transport and supply need to be well planned out, with centralised hubs and transport partners being connected efficiently.
- The creation of legacy products is an idea that ancipreneurs can explore to attract customers with a weakness for aesthetically pleasing items.

Activity 1: What kind of legacy products could you offer your loyal customers? Could you think of a reward or a loyalty program for your brand? What are the steps that you would chalk out to map out an exclusive program for your high-ticket clients?

Activity 2: Make a chart of all raw materials that are being used for your products and explore whether the waste generated could be recycled and reused for optimum resource utilisation.

CHAPTER 8

ANCIENT CHINESE WISDOM FOR ENTREPRENEURS

Ancient Chinese philosophers regarded "uncertainty" or "ambiguity" as a way of life, and the three pillars supporting this theory are "Tao," "Yin-Yang," and "Wu" concepts. "Tao" refers to a perpetual state of "becoming" where the destination might be known, but the nature of the roads and the various interactions and events leading up to the state of the "being" are unknown and, thereby, beautiful learning experiences.

"Yin-Yang" represents paradox—a battle of contradictions and complementarities that inspired Neils Bohr's famous wave-particle duality theory. The balance of the opposites can be brought about by acceptance, appreciation and level-headed resolution of paradoxical business challenges like competition-cooperation, exploration vs exploitation, globalisation vs localisation issues, etc. "Wu" theoreticians are advocates of intuitive imagination for problem-solving with foresight.

"If you think in terms of a year, plant a seed; if in terms of ten years, plant trees; if in terms of 100 years, teach the people."

Portrait of Confucious. Painting by Chinese School. Copyright: Bridgeman Images

Confucius, who is widely considered to be China's first great philosopher and lived from 551 to 479 B.C.E., was revered by many experts. The Analects saved the knowledge of Confucius that his students reported. Confucius's perspectives were further developed by other great Chinese philosophers like Mencius and Xunzi. During the Neo-Confucian period of 960 to 1279, his ideas were rediscovered and popularised. According to Confucius' teachings, learning was essential for personal growth and advancement.

Confucianism is an invaluable code of ethics for managing a business because it aligns with accepted professional practices and calls for companies to be beneficial to society, making use of hierarchy and empowering moral leaders. Moreover, the "golden rule" of treating others as one wishes to be treated and emphasising virtues are critical for corporate success.[63, 64, lxiii, lxiv, lxv, lxvi, lxvii]

"Guanxi," a Chinese term, stands for "relationships," and these relationships play an essential role in the business world. Business conducted in China is based on mutual favours that are done out of goodwill and with the expectation that they will be continued. The concept of respect in a business setting anchors this ideology. As Confucius once said, let us take the Chinese business culture as an example and show respect to everybody with whom we do business.

"Without feelings of respect, what is there to distinguish men from beasts?"

Attaining the status of Junzi is deemed to be the highest accomplishment in Confucianism. Junzi is the term used to refer to the perfect leader in Confucianism, and the concept is still applied in businesses today. Those in high positions of power are respected as Junzis since they act as exemplary role models. For a person to display integrity, they must act selflessly and lead by example. If they are seen as a leader who upholds strong moral values, then people will trust them wholly.

According to Confucius, learning involves not only the acquisition of theoretical knowledge but, even more importantly, the capacity to use this information in actual scenarios. Confucius's texts make it clear that this type of skill can only be developed when one knows which feelings to be having at the appropriate moments, and these kinds of emotions can only come after going through a process involving music, rituals, role-modelling, and more—which ultimately shapes both the student's body and mind.

Confucian and Daoism principles for personality development

According to Confucious, "Life is simple, but we insist on making it complicated." As a leader, we shouldn't be complicating and obscuring things more than necessary for our job. Complicated messages can cause confusion, which slows down progress. Keeping your message and communication clear and simple will help move your organisation forward.

For example, Steve Jobs, founder of Apple, says, "*That's been one of my mantras—focus and simplicity. Simple can be harder than complex; you have to work hard to get your thinking clean to make it simple.*"

The biggest accomplishment we can make is not in preventing mistakes but in learning from them and getting back up. It's not about falling down that matters; it's how you rise again and continue forward. Everyone appreciates a comeback story. Prepare for disappointment. Give priority to recovering from your setbacks. Your ability to recover from failure, instead of the failure itself, will be judged. The world is filled with noise. Utilising silence can reveal the truth, spark ideas, calm disagreements, and open up people's emotions.

According to Confucius, recognising our lack of knowledge can help us learn what we need to know. As a leader, it is not expected for you to be an expert on everything. You should make an effort to identify, hire, utilise, and promote people who are smarter than yourself. Remain composed when everything is falling apart around you. Without maintaining control, your team won't have faith in your leadership. Creating solutions will be difficult. Expect to make more mistakes. Fear will arise in people.

> *"By three methods we may learn wisdom: first, by reflection, which is noblest; second, by imitation, which is easiest; and third by experience, which is bitterest."*

According to Confucian values, businesses should focus on building up their 'social capital.' Employees are an invaluable asset. By sharing a commitment to the company's mission or market objectives, employees throughout the company should see themselves as unified and work together. By concentrating on these objectives, everybody on the team has the chance to contribute, though in diverse methods. Working together, they can develop innovative ideas within the company.

The essential concepts of this perspective on social capital can be summarised as follows:

- All different values and beliefs are linked to form a complete circle.
- According to Confucianism, opposing points of view should not be immediately dismissed as we look for commonalities and enhancements between them. It encourages us to analyse how different elements can work together in order to better promote innovation.

Continuing with the flow of notions in personality development, it is notable that harmony and holism are prime values of Daoism. People should live and work together with all points of the environment. Acquiring knowledge in the tradition of Taoism strives to understand the Dao, which is the primary force or method of nature. How can nature reach a unified steadiness between its different powers; how can one assimilate with nature? Such exploring is a way of studying ecology. It needs patience, not indolence. Someone must be able to perceive the surroundings and all its connections so effortlessly that it will appear effortless to an onlooker. In essence, Daoists portray this process as "not doing" (Wu Wei). The student anticipates arriving at a higher level where they innately trust in their capacity to completely comprehend the ecosystem. In today's terms, this includes being aware of environmental alteration, which is an intrinsic element of a business firm's economy (demand and supply) and technology.

Through this all-encompassing and intense form of learning, new concepts can come to life.

Stephen Mitchell, a translator of the timeless Daoist masterpiece Tao Te Ching, proclaims that "Retaining receptivity gives birth to creativity. In actuality, both the creative and the receptive are elements of the same practice."

As Winefreda Asor points out in her book *Entrepreneurship in the Philippine Setting*, "The most normal means of creating ideas is like this: Have an awareness for everything."

According to Daoism, taking time to nurture yourself both physically and mentally is essential to being able to take care of others. To preserve our energy, we need to engage in personal growth and gain an in-depth understanding of the fundamental ideas of Daoism. First, we must control our cravings (body) and wants (mind) and concentrate on what is most vital to us. In this case, having a humble attitude is essential. Additionally, meditating can help us to be more focused and clear our minds of negative thoughts and feelings, which ultimately restore our energy levels.

Cultivating yourself physically and mentally can be more beneficial. When we're more in balance and less overwhelmed with emotions such as anxiety, anger and worry, it makes us more able to stay focused and productive. Acknowledging that conditions are only temporary gives us a more positive outlook and viewpoint. To focus on the more important aspects, rather than worrying too much about current situations and getting overwhelmed by details, we can concentrate on the bigger picture. Knowing the 'logic' of reversion and circularity raises our awareness of the impacts and connections of our actions, cultivating a more serious mindset.

Let us contemplate these concepts by the example of Winston Churchill. With unwavering dedication, he became a quintessential workaholic, dedicating his life towards leading the United Kingdom in World War II. Despite facing the daunting challenge of pneumonia not once but twice, he remained unfazed and never skipped a single beat. In an instant, a glaring realisation strikes us—energy reigns supreme! As entrepreneurs, we're hardwired to equate time with moolah. Although it holds some truth, let's shift our focus to the undeniable fact that energy is perhaps our most valuable resource yet!

As a beacon of leadership, it's our duty to radiate positive energy and create a ripple effect. Care for your vitality, monitor its fluctuations, and master the art of fuelling up while ditching negativity. Churchill's unwavering focus on what truly matters is a testament to the power of mental stamina. It goes on to prove that having unrelenting energy can make or break one's ability to stay mentally fortified during even the toughest of circumstances.

Learning from the art of warfare

Sun Tzu, a military general from 722–481 BC, composed 13 chapters dealing with aspects of warfare, from tactics to using spies, and shaped them into a book, *The Art of Warfare*. His intent was not to glorify violence but instead to view it as a necessary evil that should be avoided if possible.

> *"If you know both yourself and your enemy, you can win a hundred battles without jeopardy."*
>
> — **Sun Tzu**

Sun Tzu advises that understanding yourself, your enemy, and their strengths and weaknesses is the key to success in battle. Concealment from your adversary is essential, as reflected in the adage that "all warfare is based on deception." In order to prevail, it is important to appear helpless during offensive strikes, deactivate strength when in use and appear distant when near. On the other hand, when far away, we should make the enemy think we are close by. These tactics have been greatly relevant to leaders such as Mao Zedong and General Douglas MacArthur, leading to hundreds of different Sun Tzu titles on the market.

Many Japanese businesses have made this business book compulsory reading for important executives, as it teaches lessons about corporate strategy and office politics. This topic has been widely discussed in legal books, articles on the trial process, negotiation tactics and trial strategies and even in educational fields.

Bill Belichick, who has won the Super Bowl 8 times, applied lessons from it to gain insights for game prep. The Australian cricket team have mentioned the ancient work as having an impact, and Louis Felipe Scolari had his World Cup 2002 squad study it during their successful tournament.

In the book, one of the lessons says, "Whoever is first in the field and awaits the coming of the enemy will be fresh for the fight; whoever is second in the field and has to hasten to battle will arrive exhausted." In this analogy, the marketplace is represented by the field. It is essential to get your product out into the market before your competitors.

For example, understanding the need for cars that don't emit carbon and use renewable energy sources, Elon Musk founded the business, Tesla. Other car brands did not believe that electric cars would be successful. The Tesla Model S sold almost double the amount of cars in comparison to the Mercedes-Class S during the third quarter of 2016. Tesla was the first one, so Mercedes had to rush to catch up.

> "*Speed is the essence of war. Take advantage of the enemy's unpreparedness; travel by unexpected routes and strike him where he has taken no precautions.*"

The above quote resounds with the war tactics of the Mongolians. Soldiers honed their discipline and toughness with rigorous traditional hunts, always ready even in peacetime. Through their sharp hunting skills, soldiers could maintain themselves on the battlefield, forgoing traditional supply lines to sustain their long campaigns. Equipped with lightweight armour, Mongol forces possessed incredible swiftness and manoeuvrability in contrast to their heavily armoured adversaries! Commanders of the Mongolian army boldly crafted brilliant military strategies utilising astute reconnaissance and analysis of enemies' potency and alignment. The mighty Mongol forces had an unparalleled ability to engage in simultaneous battles on multiple fronts! Even in bitterly cold winters, they could zoom across vast distances, utilising frozen rivers like expressways to suddenly appear in towns hugging their banks. With expert mastery of hydrological engineering, the Mongols used it as an impressive and strategic weapon in wartime. Genghis Khan unleashed his might and built a flotilla of barges to keep the Shah's forces from escaping across the river during his assault on the Khwarazmian Empire. With ground-breaking engineering feats, the siege warfare was powered up by the creative efforts of carpenters, engineers and troops—from using ramps and dams to strategically deployed artillery.

> "*Know the enemy and know yourself; in a hundred battles, you will never be in peril.*"

This maxim stresses that understanding a business's own strengths and weaknesses, as well as those of its competitors, requires the use of business intelligence.

A perfect example is the burger wars between McDonald's and Burger King. The latter chose to challenge McDonald's and its well-known French fries by creating a better version of them and promoting them to potential customers. After becoming aware of this, McDonald's CEO quickly sent a letter to their restaurants informing them that Burger King was going to launch an attack on one of their most treasured products—their fries. The letter then provided detailed instructions on how to guarantee customers would receive high-quality fries. By utilising their knowledge of what their competition was up to, McDonald's came out on top in that battle.

Brand wars have always been about how quickly and intelligently one company responds to the jibes of the other through intelligent advertising as well as innovation that attracts customers.

Adaptability and importance of strategising

Adaptability forms an important part in the construction of the core matrix for the business principles of Fan Li, an entrepreneur in ancient China, who laid emphasis on the act of knowing others and the circumstances properly before strategising.[lxviii] In fact, Chinese culture boasts of thirty-six stratagems that have been handed down to their entrepreneurs almost since time immemorial, which help them to manage the day-to-day business with key insights and learnings from history.[lxix] The skills of adaptability help in avoiding pitfalls, reconnoitring the circumstantial landscape, and neutralising possible dangers. Ancient Chinese Strategies like "Kill with a borrowed knife," "Create something from nothing," "Hide a dragger behind a smile," "Deceive heaven to cross the sea," and "Use a woman to ensnare a man" (the beauty trap) are some of the common strategies that entrepreneurs can easily relate to the changing business environment.

As an entrepreneur, you need to be able to adapt and be flexible in your approach at all times. History has demonstrated that those who are agile and able to adapt to their environment have been much more successful than those who failed to do so.

For example, P&G could potentially repurpose their existing factories for other products or product lines when applicable. For instance, Gillette's Boston factory constructed aircraft engine components in addition to razors. Notably, the razors were critical for soldiers' kits as they ensured their gas masks could be securely fitted - just as with masks related to COVID-19 today. Adapting to customers' needs resulted in the company widening its horizons and gaining new markets. Some product lines stayed the same or grew. P&G's soap was not only popular with homemakers; it was also used by soldiers and beyond.

Consider the example of Kodak, whose founder failed to capture the growing preference towards digital photographs and thus continued to invest in expensive films and niche digitalisation, something that its competitor, Canon, was quick to adapt itself to. It also lost out on the opportunity to transform its photo acquisition site Ofoto into an Instagram precursor. It declared bankruptcy in 2012, which was attributed to its hesitant attitude towards embracing changing customer demands.

The failure of General Motors, a well-known automaker established in 1908 and a symbol of US manufacturing for over 100 years, that filed for bankruptcy protection on June 1, 2009, is a lesson here. It not only failed to adapt to customer's changing needs but did not also pay attention to Japanese rivals who came up with fuel-efficient smaller cars when oil prices spiked.

However, in the process of adapting too much to the ever-changing world, it is important not to lose your core original essence. As an example, consider the launch of the new Coke formula in 1985, which was the first time Coca-Cola tinkered with the original flavour. It upset customers so much that it was taken off the market within just seventy-nine days. This teaches us that adaptability must come with an analysis of the circumstances. If you've got a successful system that your fans love, don't mess with it! But if you're tempted to shake things up and try something new, listen to your audience's input, weigh the consequences and then decide.

If necessary, partner, merge, or ally with a competitor to join forces and create synergy in the marketplace. In order to keep up with global competition, it's important to draw in your main customers and develop any skills or technologies that could be required for success.

Insights for ancipreneurs

- Incremental learning and resilience in the face of challenges are essential attributes that can be fostered through adaptability, as previously mentioned. Through sequential deductive triangulation analysis, it has been observed that entrepreneurs who can adjust to the needs of the marketplace after failing in their first business pursuits demonstrate a resiliency to changing trends and are able to reach their goals more quickly when attempting them again.[lxx]
- To increase self-esteem with Confucian methods, one needs to prioritise learning, cultivating a hopeful outlook, adhering to Confucian beliefs, being composed in all circumstances, forming important connections and gaining the faith of family and acquaintances.
- A heightened level of awareness makes us more self-aware and attentive to everyday tasks since all actions are connected in some way. In addition, it stops us from only looking out for ourselves and discourages unethical behaviour because we are no longer preoccupied with the possibility of making money or getting something material.
- The secret to a successful work ethic is fuelling our inner fire with boundless energy and harnessing our razor-sharp mental prowess. Harnessing energy is critical, but with a finite supply each day, it's how you channel that power when you're brimming with it that's truly significant.
- Stay aware of the market's trends and shifts, and beat your competitors to the punch by introducing new products first. You have to adapt or change to keep up with the ever-changing world of business.

- Enhancing business receptivity is not only possible but can be done through techniques such as seminars, surveys, focus groups, internet consumer forums, domestic and global research teams which bridge different types of leadership, and brainstorming sessions.

Activity: Make a list of brand battles that have intrigued you in the past decade. Note down in detail the challenges posed and the witty responses issued in the clash of rivals. In the following space, certain visual cues have been provided. Find out about these advertisements and their impact.

CHAPTER 9

INSPIRING LESSONS FROM THE GREATEST LEADERS IN HISTORY

Develop emotional intelligence like Abraham Lincoln

Abraham Lincoln was one of the most exceptional and charismatic presidents of the United States, who set wonderful precedents for his successors to emulate. Abraham Lincoln's Gettysburg Address of 1863 is the most widely quoted speech in American history. His words still have relevance today, especially when it comes to marketing strategy and planning.

According to Lincoln, it is wise to take the time to prepare before taking on a task: "Give me six hours to chop down a tree, and I will spend the first four sharpening the axe."

Marketers should realise that taking the time for thorough preparation reduces the effort needed to carry out a task. Furthermore, Lincoln showed us that quality is more important than quantity when it comes to work hours and tasks. Concentrating on significant projects and campaigns will yield better results for your brand, as well as lead to greater success in your professional life.

Historical examples, such as Abraham Lincoln's speeches, demonstrate the importance of connecting to the public through poetic and clear language that allows people to feel as if they are listening to a sincere account. Successful leadership in both business and politics requires one additional, often overlooked factor. As a leader, it is important to take time to rest and recharge so that you are prepared for the challenges ahead. During his time in Washington, Lincoln visited the theatre approximately one hundred times. Even though he had bouts of sadness, he possessed a brilliant wit and could keep his audience in stitches with his anecdotes.

Source: Library of Congress, Getty Images, Credit: Fletcher C Ransom

To ensure that everyone feels part of the success, it's important to create an atmosphere where team members can share credit. To foster a positive atmosphere, it is important to accept responsibility for your mistakes as well as the mistakes of those you manage. Lincoln accepted accountability for his choices, and he attributed successes and failures to the whole team, which endeared him to many.

As a leader, you need to be ready to take charge and make decisions when voting results in a deadlock. For instance, Lincoln endured months of arguments among his cabinet regarding the abolishment of slavery before he finally made the call. After much consideration, he decided to make a landmark announcement that would free the slaves—the Emancipation Proclamation. After gathering the cabinet, he informed them that his decision had been made and didn't require any input—but would appreciate hearing their ideas on how to best implement it and its timing. Although not everyone agreed with Lincoln's choice, they appreciated that their voices had been taken into consideration. In fact, Lincoln heeded the advice of one of his cabinet members to hold off issuing the proclamation until there was a victory on the field.

He had the emotional intelligence to convert rivals into supporters through humility, grace and a cooperative attitude. For instance, William Seward was a tough opponent, but after personally meeting Lincoln, he wrote to his wife that Lincoln was unlike any man that he had met. Similarly, he deliberately introduced Edwin Stanton into his cabinet as secretary of war, knowing well about his temperament, which was so different from his own. The mutual opposites balanced each other, resulting in more prudent decisions. Lincoln was more forgiving when it came to punishing soldiers who fled from battle, compared to Stanton, who was determined to enforce discipline.

During the 2008 election cycle, CBS interviewer Katie Couric posed a question to then-candidate Barack Obama: apart from the Bible, what one book would he bring with him to the White House? He referred to Doris Kearns Goodwin's biography "Team of Rivals," which details Abraham Lincoln's command during the Civil War. Obama's decision indicated that he intended to follow the same leadership style as his predecessor from Illinois during the crisis. Indeed, the world has seen how Obama adopted Lincoln's method of inviting his most capable rivals to join his cabinet.

Effective communication is the key to success

If there's anything that history has taught us, it is that excellent oratory and listening skills are essential for any entrepreneur worth his salt.

During his Fireside Chats of the 1930s and 1940s, President Roosevelt spoke to the American people to assure them and to prepare them for the potential conflict with foreign powers in Europe and Asia.

During the Cold War, President John F. Kennedy faced one of the most nerve-wracking situations known as the Cuban Missile Crisis. In order to make the right decision regarding the Soviet Union's dealings in Cuba, President Kennedy wanted to hear the different opinions of his advisors. His experience was amplified by reading Barbara Tuchman's book on how leaders can make wrong decisions and start a conflict without wanting it. Kennedy's commitment to having independent authority is a way of avoiding bad choices.

Martin Luther King Jr. was a Baptist pastor and civil rights leader who spearheaded the movement for equality in the US. From a marketing point of view, King emphasises the importance of a clear brand identity and demonstrating faith in it in order to

Source: https://daily.jstor.org/tag/martin-luther-king-jr/

attract customers. The iconic "I Have a Dream" speech delivered by Martin Luther King Jr. is still renowned throughout the world. This picture was obtained from the Hulton Archive and was taken on Aug 28, 1963.

We can equate the well-known impact with going viral. Content that captures the attention of its viewers tends to spread quickly online. To learn the principles of marketing from Martin Luther King Jr, one should strive to communicate their message concisely and effectively. Speak in a language that is comprehensible. Martin Luther King Jr.'s "I Have a Dream" speech is shorter than an hour. The total time was 17 minutes, and it led to a momentous shift in history. It utilised several powerful rhetorical devices like metaphors, the Jeremiad (a kind of sermon for igniting moral values), as well as Aristotle's concept of pathos and ethos.

The Napoleonic strategies of leadership
New mantras of preparedness for the budding entrepreneur

Napoleon was skilled at capitalising on his strengths to gain an advantage. He would engage in combat whenever he believed he could gain the upper hand. He was an advocate of "*On s'engage, puis on voit,*" which translates to "We go into it, and then we'll see." He had the ability to be nimble in the implementation of his strategies, allowing him to quickly adapt without too much rigid planning. Napoleon broke from traditional warfare styles and methods, even when leading his troops in battle. Whenever an opportunity to gain an advantageous position presented itself, he took it. Napoleon's generals were amazed by his battle stratagems, which proved successful in the Battle of the Pyramids, where his French force of 20,000 triumphed over a Mamluk army numbering 60,000.

Napoleon's second military maxim states, "In forming the plan of a campaign, it is requisite to foresee everything [the enemy may do] and to be prepared with the necessary means to counteract it. Plans of campaign may be modified, ad infinitum, according to circumstances."

A leader should always be proactive in exploring new methods of completing tasks. In the business world, where there is constant competition, it is best to never rely on just one strategy for any given situation. If the same techniques are consistently repeated in a given situation, predictability increases, and any potential advantage you had may be eliminated as your adversaries will become more adept at guessing your next move. In the Battle of the Pyramids in Egypt, The French had a ratio of 1 to 3 against them. Despite the Mamluks incurring 6,000 casualties, Napoleon's tactical prowess enabled the French to suffer only 30 losses.

Boosting the team through care and rewards

After receiving assistance from others, Napoleon especially took the time to show gratitude. No matter the form—verbal praise, monetary reward, or through granting medals—Napoleon always expressed his gratitude to those who fought for France. In 1802, Napoleon created the "Legion Of Honour" as a way to honour citizens and soldiers for their services, a tangible recognition of merit.

Napoleon famously declared, *"You call these baubles, well, it is with baubles that men are led... Do you think that you would be able to make men fight by reasoning? Never. That is good only for the scholar in his study. The soldier needs glory, distinctions, rewards."*

He was of the view that the soldiers should be given utmost attention and checked. After lining up the battalions, he advised to spend eight hours closely examining each soldier individually, addressing concerns and evaluating weapons to ensure they don't lack anything. According to him, there were numerous benefits of these seven-to-eight-hour reviews; the soldiers become acclimated to bearing arms and being on duty, which demonstrates to them that their leader deeply cares for them, which invigorates strong morale.

Being an entrepreneur today requires you to take care of the team that can make or break you by being empathetic and incentivising good conduct and service. Here, we can all take a leaf out of Napolean's book, isn't it?

Leading from the front

Napoleon's Marshals were renowned as the best generals in the world. They led their troops into countless victorious battles. Napoleon was the one managing the tactics, and he never seemed to be far from the fighting. Europe's monarchs typically abstained

Source: imago images

from engaging in combat and instead delegated the fighting to their military commanders while they remained ensconced in luxury palaces or secluded themselves away from battle. This was not Napoleon's way. Compulsively mobile, he realised that his leadership had to be felt from the front lines rather than from a stationary seat of power. He wanted to take in the battlefield firsthand in order to make real-time strategic decisions.

What number of CEOs are actively leading their troops in battle on a daily basis? How often do they communicate with customers, partners, clients and suppliers? How many of them are putting in the effort and doing the hard work? In my opinion, not many. Many are satisfied staying in their offices and conference rooms, making decisions from afar. It is not difficult to understand why so many people become lost.

David Chandler, regarded as one of the most prominent Napoleonic historians, once stated: "Napoleon was unequalled in terms of strategic planning." He utilised the outstanding manoeuvrability and enthusiasm of his armies to the fullest extent by devising two main strategic systems. When facing a stronger opponent, Napoleon would use the central position strategy to divide the enemy and take them out one at a time. On the other hand, if the foe was weaker than his forces, Napoleon would often set up an envelopment by occupying their attention with part of his army while the main force swept against their lines of communication to separate them from their supplies. Occasionally, the two strategies were utilised at once.

Starting a business often involves a lot of trial and error by throwing different products or ideas at the market to see what works. For this, there is no scientific method or thorough research, no comparison to competitors, and no intricate planning. They are desperately running with all their might, hoping that if enough things work out, they will be able to stay afloat. They may do so temporarily. It may be possible to "wing it" and be successful for a while using this approach. In the end, the company that uses a systematic approach will have the edge over one that doesn't.

It's vital to remember that Napoleon was a trailblazer. His fighting style was revolutionary compared to the norms of his era. He deployed a remarkable combination of speed, power, and groundbreaking tactics that had not been seen on the battlefield in many years. Forging ahead of your competition requires innovative thinking. How can you outpace your rivals? What approach can you take to concentrate your resources on a certain topic and maximise its impact? What tactics can you use to quickly capitalise on an opportunity with your team? Properly preparing your use of velocity, scale, and intense manoeuvres before the match begins will guarantee you can quickly act when a chance presents itself.

Learning entrepreneurship from great inventors and scientists

Thomas Alva Edison

In the 1800s, electricity was invented by Alessandro Volta, and after that both Humphrey Davy and Warren de la Rue tried making lamps for homes but could not control the brightness as well as high manufacturing costs. Thomas Alva Edison, the brilliant inventor, embarked on a daring quest to revolutionise the way we light up our homes. After tinkering with his ideas for a considerable amount of time, he realised that he required some assistance to make his dream a reality.

Source: Getty Images, Hulton Archives

In a brilliant move, he recruited a fresh-faced whiz kid straight out of Princeton University by the name of Francis Upton to assist him in his cutting-edge New Jersey laboratory. A collaborative dream team was formed as Edison, Francis, and a group of scientific minds joined forces. With immense dedication and countless trials, they experimented with 3,000 distinct designs and 6,000 diverse plants for three years, all on a mission to find the perfect bulb filament! After much experimentation and exploration, the solution was discovered in none other than the versatile and resilient bamboo plant! In 1879, Edison lit up the world with his patent and, a year later, dazzled it even further by founding the Edison Electric Illuminating Company. But here's the thing: he didn't do it alone. This visionary entrepreneur knew the power of collaboration and brought together an epic team to create something truly remarkable. They embraced the journey of collaborative work, harmoniously working together to craft a masterpiece, one electrifying innovation at a time. He was persistent enough to create a lamp that could sustain for hours, which he then proudly displayed in public in 1879. Edison always maintained that success is not always an easy journey. Sometimes, it takes 10,000 attempts to find the perfect path forward.

He also believed in hard work and perfection; as he once famously said, "Genius *is one percent inspiration and ninety-nine percent perspiration*." John Kreusi, the chief machinist, told Edison they were receiving a lot of offers to build power stations. Edison said to do nothing yet as they weren't ready. They had successfully carried out an experiment, but that wasn't enough. They needed to test each part of the system for longevity and faults before anyone else discovered it. This showed his commitment to the cause.

Edison's mind-blowing invention, the phonograph, rocked the audio recording sphere and altered it forever! This magnificent gadget boasts an intriguing history - after years of persistent tinkering, Edison refined it with dual needles, one for playback and another for recording! The magic of this wondrous device was unveiled when it was seamlessly produced for both homes and businesses in the 1890s! Edison's inventive genius didn't rest with the phonograph alone; he yearned to create a unique contraption that would enchant the eyes just as much as the phonograph enraptured the ears. In 1891, the world witnessed a mesmerising spectacle as Edison showcased his ground-breaking motion pictures. His imagination knew no bounds when it came to bringing the magic of cinema to life. Edison's repertoire was nothing short of remarkable - showcasing everything from the Boxing Gordon sisters to feline brawlers and even silver screen appearances by none other than Annie Oakley of Buffalo Bill's renowned "Wild West Show."

For entrepreneurs, it is a lesson in bracing oneself, for great ideas and inspiration are just the beginning of your journey towards success. But to turn them into a reality, you need two mighty weapons - hard work and a massive dose of action. Ignite these powers within and conquer not just the world of business but also the game of life. Achieving success demands a sacrifice, like a toll for a road trip—there's no way around it. Achieving this price requires a hefty investment of sweat, tears, and relentless passion. A worthy feat for those who are willing to give it their all!

But in spite of all the toil, if one can learn to enjoy his work, nothing seems hard. Being passionate about one's work, like Edison, is an important takeaway as he never thought he was doing a day's work, and for him, it was the joy of doing things.

Bring back the fun in your work and see the miracles happen!

Benjamin Franklin

Benjamin Franklin's legacy in American history is nothing short of remarkable—from his innovative inventions to his pioneering scientific discoveries, not to mention his distinguished political career as a statesman, and let's not forget, the man who signed America's Declaration of Independence.

Franklin's legendary status was forged through remarkable accomplishments that set him apart from the masses. From print apprentice to book mogul and paper tycoon, this individual rose to become Philadelphia's biggest bookseller and the colonies' foremost paper merchant. After bidding farewell to the world of commerce in 1748, he embarked on a journey to explore the realms of science and philosophy. And his relentless efforts were showered with recognition, as the prestigious Harvard and Yale universities conferred upon him honorary master's degrees. Not only did Franklin have a golden tongue that commanded attention, but he also had a work ethic that put even the most dedicated of us to shame. In his memoirs, this legend revealed the secret to his success—burning the midnight oil to ensure each task was not merely finished but perfected. In the bustling city of Philadelphia, Franklin's display of diligence caused quite a stir. As his reputation bloomed, customers shunned his rivals and flocked to him in droves.

Benjamin Franklin invented the lightning rod, revolutionising knowledge of electricity and storms. He was completely engrossed in the experiments leading up to it, from designing batteries to electrifying turkeys, as he wanted to make electricity useful to the masses and also prevent lightning-related deaths, which were very common and dangerous. Despite constraints, he and his son carried out their famous kite-flying incident that proved that the electrified air during a thunderstorm could transfer charge all down the twine to a metal key attached to the bottom - and the concept of the lightning rod was born. He was generous to never patent his invention as he wanted the common people to freely benefit from it.

As the apprentices in Franklin›s shop turned 21 and emerged as journeyman printers, they were granted the freedom to venture out on their own—if only they could scrape together the coin to get started. It never occurred to him that his trailblazers could potentially transform into formidable foes in the local market. Rather than just seeing it as a mere opportunity, he perceived it as a brilliant business concept. With his entrepreneurial spirit, he generously equipped them with all the necessary tools and materials, empowering them as printing partners in the thriving colonial city—filling a much-needed void that had long been neglected. As collaborators, he received a generous slice—one-third, to be exact—of their yearly earnings while also assisting in their conquest of uncharted markets, creating a win-win situation!

He broke free from the conventional and ideated a novel approach to accomplishment. With cotton rags as their raw material, he and his wife ventured into the world of paper mills and found immense success while running a flourishing wholesale paper business. After successfully conquering the issue of supply, Franklin shifted his focus to distribution, devoting long years to advocating for the most coveted position in colonial post offices. As soon as he ascended to the position of deputy postmaster, he strived for efficiency like a man possessed. With his cunning tactics, he revolutionised the delivery system between Philadelphia and New York, slashing the time taken to just one day. He also introduced two ground-breaking services - home delivery (yes, you read it right) - and a dead letter office to better manage undeliverable mail. Franklin's shrewd move of designating acquaintances and loved ones as postmasters elevated his sphere of influence, widened the reach of his publications and pumped up his personal earnings. He swiftly found himself in the midst of an intricate web of inter-colonial communication, deemed as one of the most vibrant and vigorous networks across the globe.

There are several lessons in ingenuity, perseverance, and enthusiasm to be learnt from Franklin. Entrepreneurs should learn to think out of the box and carry those ideas to fruition, and this sometimes needs to be done not just for profit but for common benefit.

Who can survive in business - Teachings from Charles Darwin

> *"It is not the strongest of the species that survives, nor the most intelligent that survives. It is the one that is the most adaptable to change."*
>
> – Charles Darwin

Charles Darwin provided us with the 'theory of evolution' by a painstaking process of experimentation and exploration that has been inspirational for several generations of scientists. During the 1880s, Charles Darwin discovered 14 species of finches in the Galapagos Islands. The beak of each species evolved over time to consume the available food on their respective islands. Without this adaptation, the species would have died out.

While the journey of his findings is breathtaking, perhaps it is the teachings from the corporate world derived from Darwinian theory that are most important.

According to the theory:

> *"Variation is a feature of natural populations, and every population produces more progeny than its environment can manage. The consequences of this overproduction are that those individuals with the best genetic fitness for the environment will produce offspring that can more successfully compete in that environment. Thus, the subsequent generation will have a higher representation of these offspring, and the population will have evolved."*

Year after year, new companies and start-ups sprout like dandelions in a field. Each one hustles to stay alive amidst the fierce competition. But standing tall among them all are companies fortified with unbreakable vision, mission, and culture at the heart of their strategy - they are the real game changers! Equipped with long-term goals and a crystal ball-like ability to predict the future, these companies know how to formulate strategies that will pierce through any obstacle thrown their way. Nimble and quick-witted, they can adapt to sudden shocks and changes seamlessly - proving their worth in the long run!

Without a clear vision, solid strategy and the ability to adapt to changes, companies vanish into thin air when pitted against their competition! Amidst the wild terrain of commerce, only the boldest predators reign supreme. In a world where consumer habits are as fickle as a hummingbird's flight path, even B2B and B2C giants must adapt or become mere prey.

Take, for instance, the cases of Blockbuster and Netflix. Do you know that Blockbuster was established in 1985 as a company providing VHS rentals? In the year 1999, Blockbuster became a public company with over 6,500 stores nationwide.

Reed Hastings, the founder of Netflix, was faced with a major challenge as a customer of Blockbuster. He returned the movie "Apollo 13" to Blockbuster six weeks past the due date after finishing it and was penalised for the delayed return of the movie. He vehemently opposed the notion of paying for late movie returns and stood firmly against it! In a fiery burst of entrepreneurial passion, Hastings birthed the revolutionary streaming giant known as Netflix.

Netflix caught on to the insatiable appetite of movie lovers and fulfilled their craving by delivering as many movies as they desired right at their doorstep. The roots of Netflix can be traced back to its humble beginnings as a revolutionary DVD rental-by-mail service. Then they realised that maybe physical delivery of DVDs wasn't necessary. Netflix developed an innovative idea that transformed its operational approach. A subscription-based streaming service would be initiated, offering access to movies through a computer or other compatible devices.

Netflix has become increasingly popular in the market. Hastings held the belief that selling Netflix would be profitable. Hastings, a daring entrepreneur, flipped the game on Blockbuster by boldly pitching his Netflix dream for $50 million. Blockbuster expressed amusement and stated that Netflix wasn't as popular as they thought and that individuals prefer to visit a store in person and select the DVD they desire to purchase. Hastings was left fuming, and this time, with extraordinary marketing tactics, Netflix went all in and drastically slashed prices, leaving Blockbuster gasping for air. Slowly but surely, Netflix expanded its empire of streaming enthusiasts and surpassed the once mighty Blockbuster. Blockbuster made every possible attempt to thwart Netflix's rise to the top but couldn't.

The summer of 2010 saw the downfall of the mighty Blockbuster, with it declaring bankruptcy, paving the way for a new streaming giant. Today, Netflix reigns as an internationally acclaimed brand with jaw-dropping financial success, boasting a whopping $5.8 billion annual gross profit in 2018!

This is a warning bell for business leaders. Buying habits have changed dramatically in recent years. Thanks to the mighty Internet, along with the latest social networking and mobile channels, consumers and businesses alike have transformed. The marketplace is a whole new ballgame. Buyers have more power than ever before, armed with endless information from both companies and their fellow consumers. They want to dictate when they receive information, as well as how it's presented to them.

In this ever-changing market, as we have also seen in Chapter 6, only an ancipreneur can thrive with a flexible mindset, which is a true reflection of Darwinism.

Insights for ancipreneurs

- For a successful marketing campaign, marketers must have complete faith in their message. Investing time in creating a well-crafted message yields great dividends in the long term.
- Your business should have flexible core strategies that can be used consistently. Business problems can usually be boiled down to straightforward algorithms. Figuring out which variables are profitable and which are to be eliminated or value-reduced is usually the most time-consuming part. After establishing your goals, it typically becomes easier to determine how to raise or lower them. For instance, widening your reach can result in more customers and increased sales. The success of your SEO strategy depends on what you do better than your competitors, an understanding of the strengths and weaknesses of your competition, and the budget you are working with. Identifying which levers to pull and how to go about it is the job of the business strategists of your team.
- Hard work, patience and ingenuity are the three pillars on which entrepreneurs need to base their foundation. Losing steam midway owing to obstacles is never the way out. At the same time, one needs to be critically observant to develop new solutions as well as create support networks through incentivisation and opportunities.

Activity: You're the unrivalled giant of the Internet. Opportunities present themselves to acquire ventures with

the potential to grow tremendously in the network space, and yet, as your company does not have a clear vision of its own focus points and strengths, it procrastinates on the decisions, allowing the competitors to blow off the deal. Your company neither capitalises on nor upgrades its acquired and existing ventures, allowing them to stagnate as they slowly go out of trend. How would a present-day Napoleon make a difference in this situation?

Trivia: With its debut in 1994, Yahoo became the internet oasis for news junkies, email enthusiasts and search engine connoisseurs alike - a hub of digital delight that drew in hordes of fans from far and wide. While Yahoo enjoyed a monopoly without the looming shadows of mighty Google or Facebook, it managed to snag advertisers who didn't bat an eye before whipping out their wallets. However, in this sweet spot, Yahoo failed to nurture its search feature and overlooked the potential of hiring top-notch programmers. The company's downfall could be likened to a tragic opera, with each regrettable decision adding another sombre note to the string, leading to its inevitable demise.

In a classic case of missed opportunities, Yahoo fumbled the chance to snag Google in 2002 for a paltry $1 billion. Instead, they dilly-dallied until Google's skyrocketing success pushed the price tag up to an astronomical $3 billion. Lesson learned: procrastination is pricey! Back in the late '90s, Yahoo turned a blind eye to search, believing it was merely a drop in their income bucket. Similarly, in 2006, Yahoo made a bold bid to acquire the mighty Facebook for a staggering $1 billion. However, the social media giant's leader, Mark Zuckerberg,

turned down the generous offer. Rumour has it that Zuckerberg was this close to selling out for a whopping $1.1 billion as the board's directors convinced him. However, Yahoo executives did not agree to the increased amount and thus lost the deal!

Despite acquiring Flickr in 2005, Yahoo tragically failed to steer the ship of photo-sharing towards the thriving seas of social media, resulting in a missed opportunity. Yahoo shelled out a staggering $1.1 billion for young upstart Tumblr back in 2013. Unfortunately, the investment didn't quite pan out as planned, and Tumblr went out of fashion.

Yahoo struggled with a defined company-wide purpose since the start, which led to costly regrets.

CHAPTER 10

BUSINESS LESSONS FROM HISTORICAL EVENTS

*S*tepping into uncharted waters - a new era of uncertainty and complexity awaits us as business leaders! The business climate is like a ticking time bomb. A maelstrom of supply disruption, financial instability, political tumult, and social turbulence has engulfed us, making the business landscape immensely unpredictable with little respite in sight. Here, learning from the significant events that changed world history can be a game-changer!

Planning strategies to be learnt from 'D-Day'

After years of suffering, the greatest and most ambitious undertaking of mankind forever changed the course of history - the Allied Forces liberated Europe from Nazi forces. Uniting the world's intellect and ambition like never before, the only thing more daunting than the task ahead was abandoning it - a risk too great to bear. An ambitious, sophisticated plan of action took shape involving nearly three million British, Canadian and American soldiers. When it was unleashed on D-Day (June 6th, 1944), pandemonium ensued!

The figure shows troops heading out on D-day for the invasion of Normandy. Photograph was sourced from the Guardian with credit to Bettmann/Corbis for the picture.

Foul weather delayed the operations, and still, the decision remained unchanged - the attack was inevitable. The ships arrived later than expected. Time, it seems, was not on their side. Also, the stormy waves weakened the amphibious landing forces before they reached the invasion beaches. Above the chaos of France, paratroopers scattered like confetti in a bid to dodge the azure ocean below. With communications crushed or scrambled, there was a desperate situation of life and death, where young officers and inexperienced non-commissioned officers were left with limited facts to shape the future of the globe. After months of rigorous training alongside their brothers-in-arms, battle-ready units were hurled overseas to France, where they encountered a discombobulated array of stragglers.

Despite all the planning, why was careful strategising essential during battle, and how can business leaders apply it in a mercurial market?

Forming a team, tempering egos, and practicing humility should be done as a strategic choice before a battle starts rather than when it is already chaotic. In preparation for D-Day, both Allied leadership and the troops developed an understanding of one another and recognised the importance of each person's contributions. Planning is essential to the success of any endeavour, as demonstrated by the preparations for D-Day taken by both the Axis and Allied forces. By contrast, the Axis approach saw military culture structured with a firm commitment to relying on orders, while the Allies championed an inventive and cooperative ethos. On D-Day, the tumult of progress ultimately tipped in favour of the team equipped to react with agility and inventiveness. While Axis commanders were squabbling amongst themselves, Allied leadership rolled up their sleeves and forged ahead.

Making your own luck—that's the key to success! Worried about fluctuations of fortune? It's all but a façade - chances are equalised through the world! Savvy leaders and teams seize even the tiniest opportunity to achieve success. They don't have more opportunities than others, but just know how to maximise whatever potential they have! Highly cooperative, trusted teams are primed to identify key opportunities and make quick moves! So collaborative planning sessions are a great way to build trust and gain new perspectives.

Takeaways from the rise and fall of the Ottoman Empire

The Ottoman economy sure knew how to thrive! With the Sultanate's guidance in advancing their exports and the innovative merchant houses taking calculated risks for unexplored trade

Source: https://mvslim.com/a-story-of-two-civilisations-brief-history-of-islam-and-the-west-book-extracts/

ventures, luxury goods were imported and exported with captivating finesse. This gave these merchants a tremendous seat at the table of international markets and politics. In Ottoman society, liberal economic principles combined with social justice in the distribution of income.

Trading hadn't just stayed in one place. It zoomed across cities and into distant realms, connecting merchants and craftsmen alike! A "chain of exchange" was formed between business-based households as they communicated and traded goods, effectively creating an intricate social network! Merchants needed partners to help them fund market trades, reducing their risk of financial loss. They sourced investors from other successful merchants. This allowed them to maximise profits and form lasting friendships, which helped them build a network of contacts that could secure reliable goods and valuable trading opportunities. Risk-sharing agreements were essential in an unstable economic climate, providing security and diversity.

The merchants of Ottoman society faced many hazards when travelling away from their well-known bases for trade. For safety, they used caravanserai, which were small inn-like outposts situated along major trading routes. Thus, these became a vital hub of exchange: interconnections of trade through which materials ranging from sugar to coffee to pepper, tobacco and silk meandered

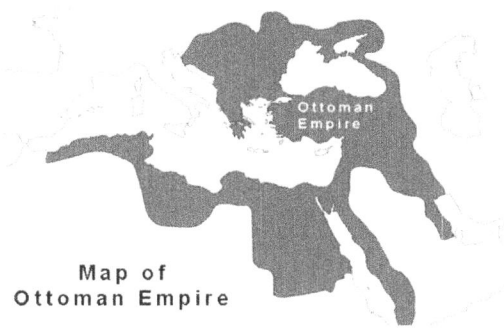

Map of Ottoman Empire

throughout the empire. The place of the market controllers was taken over by guilds, creating a safe haven for both quality work and control of pricing. Members could no longer be taken advantage of by price gouging from elitists, and more predictability was introduced to the supply and demand cycle. Through efforts such as regulating prices and standardising quality, stability was brought back to a sometimes volatile atmosphere.

Despite their heavy reliance on agriculture, the Ottoman Empire was no match for Europe's booming technological and economic advances; European goods proved to be both higher in quality and cheaper in price, virtually eliminating the Ottoman economy from competitive markets. And with volatile weather events that caused serious economic disruption, it seemed as though the already shaky foundations of the empire were heading down a one-way path to collapse.

The Ottoman Empire was bogged down by a weakening economy: the unfair "capitulations" system, bribed inefficiencies, small farmers stifled by large landowners and frequent wars decimating trade. European powers inched closer and closer to international commerce; corruption ran rampant, and power accumulated in few hands. All these factors crumbled the Ottoman Empire's potential for economic expansion. Across the board, there was chaos- ineffective military action and random policy formation. The masses shied from reform of antiquated systems like transport, media and the army- calling them 'ungodly innovations. Discrimination among loyal subjects meant that only those armed with bribery, nepotism and favouritism could climb to higher echelons in office, not a strategy for finding qualified leaders! This mishandled of power set a chain reaction into motion- leading to lands being lost due to weak armies, economic struggles and other powerful countries on the rise. To really sum it up, geographical difficulties, abolishment of 'devsirme' army forces, and de-secularisation signalled the end of this powerhouse empire!

What entrepreneurs can learn from revolutions around the world?

When we look towards history for lessons in managing our businesses, we tend to overlook the events that have shaped our society. Why are we as privileged as we are today? Who were the people who fought for our rights? Why did the need arise for them to do so?

The answers lie in the revolutions that broke the reign of monarchies and overthrew colonial empires. Let us have a bird's eye view of these revolutions and what they can teach us.

The French Revolution

In pre-1789 France, society had three groups. People involved in church matters were called the clergy, and they were part of the first estate. The second estate was made up of important figures in state administration, like nobility, and both estates got all the privileges from birth and were even free from paying taxes to the state. Unfortunately, the third estate was a mismatched bunch, which included big businessmen, court officers, lawyers, artisans, peasants, servants, and landless labourers who bore the heavy burden of taxes.

Due to multiple wars, the State treasury was depleted during Louis XVI's reign. The precarious situation was further complicated, with France dabbling in the American War of Independence, coupled with a failed taxation system. As the elite sat back and enjoyed their endless riches, those of the Third Estate were forced to bear the weight of tax after tax until they could shoulder it no longer.

Louis XVI, the Bourbon king of France, was known for leading a life of luxurious excess and exhibiting autocratic tendencies, which were often coupled with a perceived lack of assertiveness. The masses were left disillusioned as their lives became engulfed in abject poverty and pervasive hunger, leaving them to weather an unrelenting storm of misery. As the winds of change blew through society, the middle class clamoured for fiscal and judicial reform to propel progress forward. However, the stubborn nobles clung to their cherished privileges from the outdated system, turning a blind eye to the needs of their fellow people.

Tension flared up between the three groups of the society as repeated voting processes led to no result, and this led to revolutionary fervour burning throughout the country with military coups ('The Storming of The Bastille', nobility fleeing the country as peasants burnt their homes ('The Great Fear'), arrest and execution of the king and queen followed by violent activities by extremists on nobles accused of treason ('The Reign of Terror').

The motto of 'Liberty, Equality, Fraternity' swept through the land and gave way to constitutional reforms.

Source: *Coloured print of French Revolution poster edited by Paul André Basset, Public Domain Stock Images*

As we have seen from previous instances in history, mismanagement of funds in the company to benefit just the top rungs of the hierarchical ladder can have an immense negative impact on the business. There's a reason why negotiations with the employee unions are deemed to be extremely important and sensitive. Entrepreneurs cannot expect to sit in a board room and make decisions along with a few key members that would affect lots of other lives that serve their business. All voices must be heard and taken into consideration. Disparity in the treatment of groups within your team based on wealth and social status could lead to dissatisfaction that can be detrimental to progress.

The American Revolution

The American Revolution occurred due to colonial rebellion against British attempts to exert more control over the colonies and require them to repay for the crown's defence following the

French and Indian War. The laws and taxes imposed by Britain, including the Sugar Act, Stamp Act, and Intolerable Acts, were deeply disliked.

The British forces outnumbered the revolutionaries and were more organised and disciplined with better resources. Still, the strategies adopted by the Americans were fuelled by patriotism, intelligence and sheer bravery. How else can one explain the early wins at the Battle of Lexington and Concord? The Americans showed levels of preparedness that the Britishers could not have imagined. They forced the Britishers to wade through waist-deep Brackish waters only to find their opponents waiting at the bank. The change of course to Concord did not fare well, as American snipers from their strategic positions shot down British officers before they brought in reinforcements.

Now, let's focus on the lessons applicable to us. The cutthroat world of business has turned into a global race, where you're pitted against sprightly competitors who move at an ungodly pace and wield formidable resources that could make you feel dwarfed. This has the potential to plunge one into a pit of despair. Successful entrepreneurship requires dealing gracefully with the unexpected twists and turns that come one's way. For the bold and daring entrepreneur, what innovative tactics can be deployed to reign victorious in today's business realm?

Winning in any situation requires identifying your strengths and weaknesses. Take the lead by discovering what sets you apart from your competition. What can you do that they can't? Speedy decision-making can tip the scales in your favour, especially when facing bureaucracy. Show them what you're made of, and capitalise on your ability to make bold choices!

Entrepreneurs would do well to learn from the lesson of Benedict Arnold. He had led many wars to victory under the banner of the American Revolution, but his need for extravagance, the pressing need for money to pay off his dues, the growing dissatisfaction towards his fellowmen, and the instigation of his wife, who favoured the Britishers, caused him to betray the cause of the Americans and reach out to the British intelligence. He was caught, court-martialled and to this date, to call someone a "Benedict Arnold" means that someone has committed treason of the highest order. When faced with any situation such as this, a leader and a company must ask themselves how they will overcome it. Entrepreneurs must first perform risk analysis as to what information has been leaked and which avenues it could potentially affect. The next step would be to conduct damage control by first checking further leaks of sensitive information, then identification of trouble-shooters within the company who could take action where needed. Finally, orienting the workforce towards loyalty through meetings, discussions, and incentives would be a wonderful step.

Washington Crossing Delaware, Picture by Emanuel Leutze's 1851, Creative Commons, Wikipedia

The Americans suffered losses as the British troops chased them out through New York and New Jersey in a series of battles, and all seemed lost. What happened next is an important entrepreneurial lesson. When Washington made the bold decision to cross the Delaware on ice, he had just lost several key battles, and much of the world thought the colonists' little revolution was almost squashed. But he crossed it anyway, and it changed the war as he captured 1000 prisoners in a single night and kept his army safe. You've got to be the first to believe in your ideas, your team, and the direction your company is headed long before anyone else and take bold action.

Even when Washington knew the war was slowly turning in the colonists' favour, he wasn't satisfied with just playing it safe. Instead, he made a bold move requiring his entire army to be vaccinated against smallpox. Why? Because disease was the real killer on the battlefield, not injury. This innovative decision may have been the key to winning the war and securing independence for America.

Assessing a situation and taking control of it to curtail losses and transform them into wins in the face of restricted resources and formidable opponents sums up the lessons from the American Revolution.

The Indian freedom struggle

India's freedom struggle has great lessons for modern modern-day entrepreneurs. It never fails to amaze how a nation so diverse in its geographical, demographical and behavioural attributes across the landscape could rise unitedly against the formidable East India Company that had the hearty support of the mighty British empire. The 'divide-and-rule' policy eventually did not work out for British Imperialists as men and women shed their distinctions of caste and religion to rise as a whirlwind.

However, the freedom fighters were scattered, of different mindsets, and backgrounds, and often disagreed with each other. For instance, the extremists Lal, Bal, Pal, as they are fondly called (Lal Bahadur Shashtri, Bal Gangadhar Tilak, Bipin Chandra Pal) wanted to continue on their path of blowing up assemblies and snatching freedom through a blood-stained path. For them, the sufferings of their countrymen had tried all their tolerance levels, and they wanted an eye for an eye. On the other hand, moderates like Gopal Krishna Gokhale wanted to follow official protocols and achieve peace talks with the British by orienting public opinion, writing letters to the Crown, foreign correspondences, etc. They believed in less "barbaric means" so that the British would take note of the grievances and work towards development as well as collaborate on the idea of freedom. These differences in ideologies led to the Surat split in 1907. Mahatma Gandhi's non-violent policy had its share of supporters and nay-sayers.

There have been several instances of differences between Subhas Chandra Bose and Mahatma Gandhi, Jawaharlal Nehru and Sardar Patel, B.R Ambedkar and Mahatma Gandhi, and many others.

Every freedom fighter, though, had something important to contribute. The verbal and physical attacks by the extremists showed our courageous mettle to the Britishers, and they realised that violence would be met by violence if they did not stop exploiting Indians. Constant paperwork by the moderates, along with demand for discussions by the moderates and critical thinkers, prepared the world's public opinion against British oppression and forced them to pause in their tracks. Mahatma Gandhi's Dandi March, non-violent protests by fasting and *dharnas*, gained momentum and took them by surprise. The company officials were at a loss as to how to deal with his unique way of protesting. Even the women under the leadership of Kasturba Gandhi took part in the protests where they burnt Britain-manufactured clothes and products, advocating the cause of 'Swadeshi.' The approaches might have been different, but in one way or the other, all of them were fighting for their motherland.

When building a team and working towards a common goal—say, launching a product, reworking brand identity or researching growth avenues, an entrepreneur cannot expect that all the team members would think alike or be supportive of one another. Each employee is unique and brings a fresh perspective to the table. Here, it is important to lend everyone an ear and allow them the space to utilise their capacities to the fullest for the common target. Leaders should refrain from comparisons and segregation and rather encourage employees to embrace their exclusive creative sides by working together but from different angles.

Insights for ancipreneurs

- Unlock the secrets of the rebels and revolutionise your mindset! Unleash your inner innovator by exploring uncharted territories. First, scope out the competition and then chart your own course. According to the renowned speaker and wordsmith Joel Weldon, one must take a detour from the conventional path of following others and instead blaze their own trail. After all, being a leader is much more thrilling than following suit!
- The final choice comes down to greatness and glory or mediocrity and defeat. In the business world or on the battlefield, there's a thin line between these, and it all depends on whether you can unlock possibilities, strategise effectively, and seize the initiative while not getting bogged down by challenges.
- Ideological opposites come together in corporate settings, creating a stimulating blend of conservative and liberal thought! Traditionalists stick to the tried-and-true approach, while innovators are constantly exploring new possibilities. It is important to respect the diversity in the workforce and capture its potential for the future of the company.
- Do not try to change the entire cultural space of the company or the production unit that your business has acquired. For smooth transitions and to earn the loyalty of new employees as well as suppliers, one has to allow space for the existing cultural practices of the employees to continue so that they can familiarise themselves with the new roles comfortably.

Activity: In the previous two chapters, we discussed some dazzling events and personalities in history with the power to inspire change in entrepreneurial thinking. It's time for you to put yourself in their shoes and list down how/why you would do things differently or exactly the same! Do include more examples from world history in the following list.

Historical Event/ Person	What should you do like them?	Which of their mistakes would you never repeat?

CHAPTER 11

CONCLUSION

$\mathcal{A}$s we reach the end of this book, it is important for the 'ancipreneurs' to ponder upon what they can do differently by learning from historical evidence, how they can reshape their mindsets and why there is a need to pay heed to ancient words of advice. This book is aimed at opening up critical thinking avenues amongst the business leaders of tomorrow.

It is vital that business leaders ask themselves these questions after exploring examples from the annals of history in this book. Does your organisation embrace a flat organisational structure, or are you open to exploring new ways of thinking? Are you open to potentially encountering failure while striving for success? What ethical measures does your company have in place? Have you ensured employee satisfaction? What about risk analysis, competition management and networking? Unifying the case studies presented in this book while reflecting on these aspects can greatly help you to soar high in your arena.

Be it matters of laziness or productivity, taking risks or controlling stress, all these can be enhanced with concepts taken from antiquity that will form the thoughts of entrepreneurs

Conclusion

and help them manage their enterprises more effectively. The eternal instructions on entrepreneurship, derived from both Eastern philosophies and Western tradition, including Greek and Roman scholars, are sure to propel the freshers in the field for many future years. Additionally, reflecting on Chinese battlefield tactics, which are generally referred to as "wisdom of the East," can greatly impact entrepreneurs and give them an advantage in their business dealings. Concepts within Indian writings, as well as suggestions from Persian, Greek, and Roman intellectuals, can shape the reasoning skills of present-day entrepreneurs to achieve their tomorrow desires. Furthermore, it is hoped that the budding entrepreneurs would be captivated by Aristotle's rhetorical techniques, which contribute to establishing convictions, heightening human values, and resolving 'pain points' that modern entrepreneurs experience. It is due to associating old ideas with current demanding times that helps business owners associate better with the ever-changing professional world as they can likewise win over all people like patrons, investors, and team members with greater finesse. We have also learnt that if you want to conquer foreign markets, you can't skip the history of their culture!

Various historical accounts demonstrate distinguished figures who were able to wheel adversity into opportunities and dodge loss by using problem-solving skills paired with innovative thinking, while taking the global community into account for the benefit of the society. We have seen in the sub-chapters on revolutions as to how insight into the factors behind discrimination and inequality among individuals can prevent mistakes on the part of company owners. We have encountered examples of how institutions often find themselves in a tangled mess of tough challenges. These stubborn problem areas are like deeply embedded roots that resist any type of change if we don't approach them creatively.

When it comes to what customers claim they want versus what they actually do, history has shown us that the difference can be as stark as black and white. By examining outcomes and conducting experiments, marketing concepts can be verified by ancipreneurs over a period of time. Discovering the driving forces of success is no easy feat, but once identified, they become the guiding star to navigate through the vast seas of trends—from demand patterns to competitive actions, production costs, to product benefits.

As ancipreneurs, we can possess the unrivalled ability to dissect the nuances of human experience—analysing trend lines and time series and scoping out anomalies caused by a plethora of factors. We can weave together the intricate threads of our past into one magnificent tapestry. Learning about history can not only broaden your perspectives and enable you to view the world with greater clarity and critical thinking skills but also expand one's horizon, involving delving into the depths of social influences and legal frameworks, looking beyond just monetary gains.

We have learnt through several examples as to how understanding the formation of public opinion and its impact requires a keen insight into history's rear-view mirror. To make sound public policies and stay ahead of the game, it's crucial to have a historian's perspective—one that considers the intertwining threads of politics, economy, and society over a span of time. Only when we look at the bigger picture can we anticipate and prepare rational responses to proposed legislative actions and pressing issues. Only a skilled ancipreneur can craft corporate policies with precision with an analysis of past experiences and analogies to fit today's challenges. It also illuminates the principles that unify and sustain an organisation's identity. As the gears of business turn and time ticks away, precious corporate memories are lost. But fear not, for in the skilful hands of ancipreneurs, we can revive those forgotten stories and bring them back to life!

This book can help entrepreneurs utilise history as an amazing tool for exploring the link between social progress and its influence on both financial and nonfinancial occurrences, including various monetary models and transactions. Compared to other forms of mentorship, history provides a more accessible and cost-effective option. In addition to this, studies have demonstrated that the way companies tell their story plays a crucial role in creating a strategic vision of their past to gain a competitive edge for themselves and their key partners. By delving deeper into the ocean of historical narrations, one can find priceless pearls of wisdom!

It is important for ancipreneurs to break the mould! Don't just follow the same old routines. Aim to make things better by analysing how you work and introducing fresh ideas. Keep your standards high, but don't be afraid to think outside the box for ways to take your game to the next level - be it making little tweaks or taking big risks.

In the words of Bhagat Singh, India's famous freedom martyr, "*People get accustomed to the established order of things and tremble at the idea of change. It is this lethargic spirit that needs to be replaced by the revolutionary spirit.*"

Examining history through a bold lens helps us see the threads of constancy and moments of disruption woven throughout the ages. It is certain that implementations of ancient teachings and lessons from the past will dramatically change today's entrepreneurial attitude in a more positive direction. These words of wisdom are a legacy for all generations of business leaders, urging them to stay productive, keep up with consumers' needs and stay ahead of the competition! The 'ancipreneurial' age has arrived, and it is all yours to claim!

REFERENCES

(1) Landes, D. S.; Mokyr, J.; Baumol, W. J. *The Invention of Enterprise: Entrepreneurship from Ancient Mesopotamia to Modern Times*; Princeton University Press, 2012.

(2) *The History of the Trade and Barter System*. Square. https://squareup.com/us/en/townsquare/a-history-of-the-trade-and-barter-system (accessed 2022-12-13).

(3) Gupta, A. An Outline of Ancient Silk Route in Central Asian Region: Reference with Buddhism. *J. Adv. Humanit. Soc. Sci.* **2020**, *6* (1), 19–26.

(4) Barisitz, S. From the Beginnings to the Emergence of the Silk Road (SR). In *Central Asia and the Silk Road*; Studies in Economic History; Springer International Publishing: Cham, 2017; pp 13–48. https://doi.org/10.1007/978-3-319-51213-6_2.

(5) Zanakis, S. H.; Theofanides, S.; Kontaratos, A. N.; Tassios, T. P. Ancient Greeks' Practices and Contributions in Public and Entrepreneurship Decision Making. *Interfaces* **2003**, *33* (6), 72–88.

(6) Karayiannis, A. D. Entrepreneurship in Classical Greek Literature. *South Afr. J. Econ.* **1992**, *60* (1), 67–93.

References

(7) Bitros, G. C.; Karayiannis, A. D. Values and Institutions as Determinants of Entrepreneurship in Ancient Athens. *J. Institutional Econ.* **2008**, *4* (2), 205–230.

(8) Zanakis, S. H.; Theofanides, S.; Kontaratos, A. N.; Tassios, T. P. Ancient Greeks' Practices and Contributions in Public and Entrepreneurship Decision Making. *Interfaces* **2003**, *33* (6), 72–88. https://doi.org/10.1287/inte.33.6.72.25177.

(9) Bitros, G. C.; Karayiannis, A. D. The City-State of Ancient Athens as a Prototype for an Entrepreneurial and Managerial Society. In *Leadership through the Classics*; Springer, 2012; pp 289–304.

(10) Bitros, G. G. C.; Karayiannis, A. The Liberating Power of Entrepreneurship in Ancient Athens. *Athens Univ. Econ. Bus. Work. Pap.* **2004**, No. 155.

(11) Talaue, G. M. Aristotle's Rhetorical Triangle in Advertising: Its Influence to Saudi Arabian Consumers' Behavior. *J. Media Manag. Entrep. JMME* **2020**, *2* (2), 54–71. https://doi.org/10.4018/JMME.2020070104.

(12) Shanahan, F.; Seele, P. Shorting Ethos: Exploring the Relationship Between Aristotle's Ethos and Reputation Management. *Corp. Reput. Rev.* **2015**, *18* (1), 37–49. https://doi.org/10.1057/crr.2014.19.

(13) Simon, J. M. Aristotle's Advice for Entrepreneurs. *Big Ideas* **2015**.

(14) Triadafilopoulos, T. Politics, Speech, and the Art of Persuasion: Toward an Aristotelian Conception of the Public Sphere. *J. Polit.* **1999**, *61* (3), 741–757.

(15) Garver, E. Aristotle on the Kinds of Rhetoric. *Rhetorica* **2009**, *27* (1), 1–18.

References

(16) Rorty, A. O. *Essays on Aristotle's Rhetoric*; Univ of California Press, 1996; Vol. 6.

(17) Tarasanski, P. Metacognition, Learning, & Socrates : Asking Questions to Foster Entrepreneurial Minds. **2020**.

(18) *Business management advice: What Socrates would tell leaders | Fortune.* https://fortune.com/2020/08/25/socrates-business-management-advice-philosophy/ (accessed 2022-12-27).

(19) Ehiobuche, C.; Tu, H. DIALOGUE AS A TOOL FOR TEACHING AND LEARNING OF ENTREPRENEURSHIP. **2012**, *19* (1), 11.

(20) Dennett, P. T. A Socratic Approach to Managing Creativity in Business.

(21) Dutt, S. *Nietzsche: 5 Secrets To Become Who You Are? (7/8).* Nietzsche's Philosophy. https://medium.com/nietzsches-philosophy/nietzsches-5-secrets-to-become-who-you-are-e004841f4621 (accessed 2022-12-27).

(22) Leiter, B. Nietzsche's Moral and Political Philosophy. In *The Stanford Encyclopedia of Philosophy*; Zalta, E. N., Ed.; Metaphysics Research Lab, Stanford University, 2021.

(23) McCallum, J. S. *The Nietzsche School of Management.* Ivey Business Journal. https://iveybusinessjournal.com/the-nietzsche-school-of-management/ (accessed 2022-12-27).

(24) Nicolaides, A. Analyzing Nietzschean Virtue in Business Ethics. *J. Soc. Sci.* **2014**, *41* (2), 187–200. https://doi.org/10.1080/09718923.2014.11893355.

(25) Tajalli, P. A Nietzschean Re-evaluation of Values as a Way of Re-imagining Business Ethics. *Bus. Ethics Eur. Rev.* **2018**, *28*, 1–9. https://doi.org/10.1111/beer.12213.

References

(26) Worden, S. A Genealogy of Business Ethics: A Nietzschean Perspective. *J. Bus. Ethics* **2009**, *84* (3), 427–456.

(27) Figueira, T. J.; Brennan, T. C.; Sternberg, R. H. *Wisdom From The Ancients: Enduring Business Lessons From Alexander The Great, Julius Caesar, And The Illustrious Leaders Of Ancient Greece And Rome*; Hachette UK, 2009.

(28) Hedrick, L. *Xenophon's Cyrus the Great: The Arts of Leadership and War*; Truman Talley Books, 2007.

(29) Yenne, B. *Julius Caesar: Lessons in Leadership from the Great Conqueror*; St. Martin's Press, 2012.

(30) Caesar, J. *Commentaries on the Gallic War*; Crocker and Brewster, 1865.

(31) Barlag, P. *The Leadership Genius of Julius Caesar: Modern Lessons from the Man Who Built an Empire*; Berrett-Koehler Publishers, 2016.

(32) Whiting, K.; Konstantakos, L. *Being Better: Stoicism for a World Worth Living In*; New World Library, 2021.

(33) Sellars, J. *Lessons in Stoicism: What Ancient Philosophers Teach Us about How to Live*; Penguin UK, 2019.

(34) Coventry, P. Six Ways the Ancient Philosophy of Stoicism Can Help Business Entrepreneurs. **2016**.

(35) Sherman, N. *Stoic Wisdom: Ancient Lessons for Modern Resilience*; Oxford University Press, 2021.

(36) Stevens, R. *Stoicism for Business: Ancient Stoic Wisdom and Practical Advice for Building Mental Toughness, Productivity Habits and Success in Modern Management!*; Sophie Dalziel, 2019.

(37) Shaw, B. D. The Divine Economy: Stoicism as Ideology. *Latomus* **1985**, *44* (Fasc. 1), 16–54.

(38) Swain, T. *Way of The Stoic: Life Lessons From Stoicism to Strengthen Your Character, Build Mental Toughness, Emotional Resilience, Mindset, Self Discipline & Wisdom*; Thomas William, 2022.

(39) Bowden, H. The Ethics of Management: A Stoic Perspective. *Philos. Manag.* **2012**, *11* (2), 29–48.

(40) Jones, H. B. Marcus Aurelius, the Stoic Ethic, and Adam Smith. *J. Bus. Ethics* **2010**, *95* (1), 89–96.

(41) Pigliucci, M.; Lopez, G. *Live Like a Stoic: 52 Exercises for Cultivating a Good Life*; Random House, 2019.

(42) Robertson, D. *How to Think like a Roman Emperor: The Stoic Philosophy of Marcus Aurelius*; St. Martin's Press, 2019.

(43) Pandey, J. K. Administrative & Management Principles from Indian Scriptures: A Key of Administrative & Management Dilemmas. *Manag. Today* **2019**, *9* (1), 32–44. https://doi.org/10.11127/gmt.2019.03.05.

(44) Mukherjee, S.; Zsolnai, L. Ancient Indian Wisdom for Modern Business. In *Global Perspectives on Indian Spirituality and Management : The Legacy of S.K. Chakraborty*; Mukherjee, S., Zsolnai, L., Eds.; Springer Nature: Singapore, 2022; pp 3–14. https://doi.org/10.1007/978-981-19-1158-3_1.

(45) Misra, N. *Better Management & Effective Leadership Through the Indian Scriptures*; Pustak Mahal, 2007.

(46) Khanna, U.; Katyal, H. Role of Bhagavad Gita, Mahabharata and Ramayana in Shaping Business Management Practices. *Indian Manag.* **2017**, *1* (1), 75–84.

(47) Srivastava, S. K.; Srivastava, M.; Pandey, A.; Yadav, A. K.; Gupta, A. K. Study of Ramayana and Bhagavad Gita Technical and Managerial Intellects with Enlightening

Lessons. *Int. J. Indian Cult. Bus. Manag.* **2022**, *27* (2), 208–226.
(48) Muniapan, B. *The Bhagavad-Gita and Business Ethics: A Leadership Perspective.* Asian Business and Management Practices: Trends and Global Considerations. https://doi.org/10.4018/978-1-4666-6441-8.ch018.
(49) Basu, M. The Essentials of Organizational Management: A Study on the Bhagavad Gita. *Manag. Insight* **2019**, *15* (1), 18–28.
(50) Shah, A. K.; Rankin, A. *Jainism and Ethical Finance: A Timeless Business Model*; Taylor & Francis, 2017.
(51) Sanghavi, H. Jainism & Art of Management. *New Vistas Contemp. Manag.* 115.
(52) Inoue, S. *Putting Buddhism to Work: A New Approach to Management and Business*; Kodansha International Limited, 1997.
(53) Vallabh, P.; Singhal, M. Buddhism and Decision Making at Individual, Group and Organizational Levels. *J. Manag. Dev.* **2014**, *33* (8/9), 763–775.
(54) Weerasinghe, T. D.; Thisera, T. J. R.; Kumara, R. Buddhism and Organizational Management: A Review. **2014**.
(55) Lépineux, F.; Rose, J.-J. Spiritual Leadership in Business: Perspectives from Christianity and Hinduism. *Leadersh. Spiritual. Common Good East West Approaches* **2010**, 27–41.
(56) Porter, B. E. The Compatibility of Christianity and Business. *J. Biblic. Integr. Bus.* **1998**, *4* (1).
(57) Alserhan, B. A. *The Principles of Islamic Marketing*; Routledge, 2017.
(58) Lewis, M. K. 13. Principles of Islamic Corporate Governance. *Handb. Islam Econ. Life* **2014**, 243.

(59) Ibrahim, L.; Adamu, H. B.-Y. Participative Management: A Model of Islamic Perspective of Management (Shura) in an Organization. **2019**.

(60) Mohiuddin, M. G. Decision Making Style in Islam: A Study of Superiority of Shura (Participative Management) and Examples from Early Era of Islam. *Decis. Mak.* **2016**, *8* (4).

(61) Ntshalintshali, M.; Carmichael, T. Applicability of Shaka Zulu's Leadership and Strategies to Business. In *International Conference on Business Strategy and Organizational Behaviour (BizStrategy). Proceedings*; Global Science and Technology Forum, 2011; p 73.

(62) Allen, C. R. Shaka Zulu's Linkage of Strategy and Tactics: An Early Form of Operational Art? *MA Diss US Army Command Gen. Staff Coll.* **2014**.

(63) Smith, A.; Kaminishi, M. Confucian Entrepreneurship: Towards a Genealogy of a Conceptual Tool. *J. Manag. Stud.* **2020**, *57* (1), 25–56.

(64) Obschonka, M.; Zhou, M.; Zhou, Y.; Zhang, J.; Silbereisen, R. K. "Confucian" Traits, Entrepreneurial Personality, and Entrepreneurship in China: A Regional Analysis. *Small Bus. Econ.* **2019**, *53* (4), 961–979.

(65) Allen, L. Confucianism and Entrepreneurship in ASEAN Context. In *Entrepreneurship in Technology for ASEAN*; Springer, 2017; pp 161–173.

(66) Xiong, R.; Wei, P. Influence of Confucian Culture on Entrepreneurial Decision Making Using Data from China's Floating Population. *Soc. Behav. Personal. Int. J.* **2020**, *48* (7), 1–12.

References

(67) Zhu, Y. The Role of Qing (Positive Emotions) and Li 1 (Rationality) in Chinese Entrepreneurial Decision Making: A Confucian Ren-Yi Wisdom Perspective. *J. Bus. Ethics* **2015**, *126* (4), 613–630.

(68) Young, J. E.; Corzine, J. B. The Sage Entrepreneur: A Review of Traditional Confucian Practices Applied to Contemporary Entrepreneurship. *J. Enterprising Cult.* **2004**, *12* (01), 79–104.

(69) Romar, E. J. Virtue Is Good Business: Confucianism as a Practical Business Ethic. *J. Bus. Ethics* **2002**, *38* (1/2), 119–131.

(70) Hong, S. B. *The Business Wisdom of Ancient Chinese Entrepreneurs: Timeless Principles for Modern Times*; Partridge Singapore, 2015.

(71) Bercu, L. *The 36 Ancient Chinese Strategies for Modern Business*; Lac International Press, 2014.

(72) Lafuente, E.; Vaillant, Y.; Vendrell-Herrero, F.; Gomes, E. Bouncing Back from Failure: Entrepreneurial Resilience and the Internationalisation of Subsequent Ventures Created by Serial Entrepreneurs. *Appl. Psychol.* **2019**, *68* (4), 658–694.

WEB REFERENCES

https://www.businesswire.com/news/home/20220516005195/en/Front-Unveils-Human-Touch-a-New-Brand-Campaign-to-Inspire-Businesses-to-Bring-More-Humanity-to-Customer-Relationships

https://www.entrepreneur.com/en-in/lifestyle/part-1-6-business-sutra-and-dharmashastra-lessons-from/355331

https://ourownstartup.com/great-management-lessons-every-entrepreneur-can-learn-from-ramayana/

https://www.almendron.com/tribuna/egypts-entrepreneurs/

http://sicilycuisine.blogspot.com/2011/10/phoenicians-of-motya.html

https://www.canr.msu.edu/news/develop_the_entrepreneurship_spirit_in_you

https://gulfbusiness.com/a-brief-history-of-entrepreneurship/

https://knowledge.insead.edu/entrepreneurship/globalising-entrepreneurship-palo-alto-style

Web References

https://www.forbes.com/sites/forbeschina/2021/11/23/can-an-ancient-philosophy-help-entrepreneurs-today-social-media-helps-fuel-stoicism-renaissance/?sh=75fe6c0b4138

https://www.entrepreneur.com/leadership/success-can-come-at-any-age-just-look-at-these-6/241346

https://www.inc.com/tim-askew/great-entrepreneurship-has-divine-madness.html

https://cfe.umich.edu/know-what-you-can-control-practicing-stoicism-as-an-entrepreneur/

https://www.forbes.com/sites/forbeschina/2021/11/23/can-an-ancient-philosophy-help-entrepreneurs-today-social-media-helps-fuel-stoicism-renaissance/?sh=75fe6c0b4138

https://ckyliakoudis.com/2013/12/27/thales-philosopher-entrepreneur/

https://www.samwoolfe.com/2018/12/mythology-can-help-you-become-a-better-entrepreneur.html

https://brewminate.com/socrates-as-social-entrepreneur-what-is-poetic-truth/

https://www.alleywatch.com/2017/05/4-times-entrepreneurship-changed-course-history/

https://addicted2success.com/motivation/5-lessons-every-entrepreneur-needs-to-learn-from-julius-caesar-to-dominate/

https://medium.com/@launchyard/the-epic-for-entrepreneurs-71decd9fb064

Web References

https://strategyandstorytelling.com/blog/what-we-can-learn-from-aristotle-to-improve-pitch-performance

https://rajeevkdixit.medium.com/https-medium-com-dixiterk-14-lessons-for-an-entrepreneur-from-indian-mythology-bb74e1522acc

https://www.explorers.org/calendar-of-events/ancient-entrepreneurs-how-the-canaanites-sailed-west-and-created-the-mediterranean-trading-economy/

https://www.london.edu/think/ancient-wisdom-for-modern-business-leaders

https://www.hive.org/world/the-history-of-entrepreneurship/

https://www.nbcnews.com/id/wbna5519861

https://www.benchmarkone.com/blog/g-o-a-t-business-leaders/

https://www.cpapracticeadvisor.com/2018/05/09/ancient-advice-for-modern-business/29984/

https://www.forbes.com/sites/forbesbusinesscouncil/2021/10/18/modern-leadership-lessons-from-ancient-art/?sh=1e1f0399cb7e

https://kellercenter.princeton.edu/stories/history-entrepreneurship-goes-back-farther-you-think

https://notionpress.com/read/ancient-wisdom-for-new-age-entrepreneurs

https://sg.news.yahoo.com/7-lessons-equanimity-ancient-stoics-114500778.html?guccounter=1&guce_referrer=aHR0c

Web References

HM6Ly93d3cuZ29vZ2xlLmNvbS8&guce_referrer_sig=AQAAAJt7_V_6DNp73v0DaZckn5kHmQxLOIKHdq4hOz6OwNiIcRuH_lya4cn6jwTjwZCkvk1LDooV3b6TGVujbTrYOhl8iiYr9bppRVYDvGNsEAkzuEbhf9tNdZhXBDbhLfzPJ2z7J-b4Y1IyE2MzvJwMm43HgUFfFCVKsfQbzhO-vFi

https://hbr.org/2009/04/leadership-lessons-from-abraham-lincoln

https://buffer.com/resources/marketing-lessons/

https://www.weforum.org/agenda/2017/01/8-leadership-lessons-from-history/

https://time.com/5713400/10-lessons-history-great-leaders/

https://www.linkedin.com/pulse/20141013143619-3369121-3-business-lessons-learned-from-christopher-columbus/

https://www.linkedin.com/pulse/six-project-management-lessons-from-christopher-columbus-fritsch/

https://www.forbes.com/sites/greatspeculations/2021/10/07/what-every-aspiring-entrepreneur-can-learn-from-christopher-columbus/?sh=e3129587f208

http://www.aleanjourney.com/2019/10/5-lessons-in-leadership-effectiveness.html

https://ibecventures.com/blog/business-as-mission-leadership-lessons-from-world-war-i-remembrance-day-celebrated-100-years-ago/

https://thestrategystory.com/category/brand-marketing/

Web References

https://www.ceotodaymagazine.com/2022/07/jeff-bezos-the-inspirational-success-story-of-amazons-founder/

https://www.biznessapps.com/blog/lessons-small-business-owners-can-learn-historical-leaders/

https://www.mrjournal.ro/docs/R2/30JMR3.pdf

https://link.springer.com/chapter/10.1007/978-3-031-09349-4_10

https://books.google.co.in/books?hl=en&lr=&id=YShKAAAAQBAJ&oi=fnd&pg=PR3&dq=ancient+explorations+%2B+business+lessons&ots=tOLbyReTqa&sig=Ria9a8x5MRFicNnlSmBsFu1ILzM&redir_esc=y#v=onepage&q&f=false

https://www.eetimes.com/lessons-from-akio-morita/

https://www.entrepreneur.com/growing-a-business/akio-morita/197676

https://trak.in/tags/business/2018/08/15/5-intense-entrepreneurial-lessons-from-indias-freedom-struggle/

https://sunstone.in/blog/leadership-skills-india-freedom-fighters

https://sites.google.com/a/brvgs.k12.va.us/wh-15-sem-1-mesopotamia-fln/bartering

https://okcredit.com/blog/best-business-strategy-lessons/

https://moderndiplomacy.eu/2023/01/12/economy-of-the-ottoman-empire/

Web References

https://www.forbes.com/sites/ryanholiday/2012/05/07/9-lessons-on-leadership-from-genghis-khan-yes-genghis-khan/

https://www.entrepreneur.com/leadership/8-lessons-in-entrepreneurship-from-the-greatest-inventor-of/357161

https://www.helloprint.co.uk/blog/5-great-advertising-wars-between-big-brands/

ENDNOTES

[i] Landes, D. S.; Mokyr, J.; Baumol, W. J. *The Invention of Enterprise: Entrepreneurship from Ancient Mesopotamia to Modern Times*; Princeton University Press, 2012.

[ii] Gupta, A. An Outline of Ancient Silk Route in Central Asian Region: Reference with Buddhism. *J. Adv. Humanit. Soc. Sci.* **2020**, *6* (1), 19–26.

[iii] Barisitz, S. From the Beginnings to the Emergence of the Silk Road (SR). In *Central Asia and the Silk Road*; Studies in Economic History; Springer International Publishing: Cham, 2017; pp 13–48. https://doi.org/10.1007/978-3-319-51213-6_2.

[iv] Zanakis, S. H.; Theofanides, S.; Kontaratos, A. N.; Tassios, T. P. Ancient Greeks' Practices and Contributions in Public and Entrepreneurship Decision Making. Interfaces 2003, 33 (6), 72–88.

[v] Karayiannis, A. D. Entrepreneurship in Classical Greek Literature. *South Afr. J. Econ.* **1992**, *60* (1), 67–93.

[vi] Bitros, G. C.; Karayiannis, A. D. Values and Institutions as Determinants of Entrepreneurship in Ancient Athens. *J. Institutional Econ.* **2008**, *4* (2), 205–230.

[vii] Zanakis, S. H.; Theofanides, S.; Kontaratos, A. N.; Tassios, T. P. Ancient Greeks' Practices and Contributions in Public and Entrepreneurship Decision Making. *Interfaces* **2003**, *33* (6), 72–88. https://doi.org/10.1287/inte.33.6.72.25177.

[viii] Bitros, G. C.; Karayiannis, A. D. The City-State of Ancient Athens as a Prototype for an Entrepreneurial and Managerial Society. In *Leadership through the Classics*; Springer, 2012; pp 289–304.

Endnotes

[ix] Bitros, G. G. C.; Karayiannis, A. The Liberating Power of Entrepreneurship in Ancient Athens. *Athens Univ. Econ. Bus. Work. Pap.* **2004**, No. 155.

[x] Talaue, G. M. Aristotle's Rhetorical Triangle in Advertising: Its Influence to Saudi Arabian Consumers' Behavior. *J. Media Manag. Entrep.* **JMME 2020**, *2* (2), 54–71. https://doi.org/10.4018/JMME.2020070104.

[xi] Shanahan, F.; Seele, P. Shorting Ethos: Exploring the Relationship Between Aristotle's Ethos and Reputation Management. *Corp. Reput. Rev.* **2015**, *18* (1), 37–49. https://doi.org/10.1057/crr.2014.19.

[xii] Simon, J. M. Aristotle's Advice for Entrepreneurs. *Big Ideas* **2015**.

[xiii] Triadafilopoulos, T. Politics, Speech, and the Art of Persuasion: Toward an Aristotelian Conception of the Public Sphere. *J. Polit.* **1999**, *61* (3), 741–757.

[xiv] Garver, E. Aristotle on the Kinds of Rhetoric. *Rhetorica* **2009**, *27* (1), 1–18.

[xv] Rorty, A. O. *Essays on Aristotle's Rhetoric*; Univ of California Press, 1996; Vol. 6.

[xvi] Rorty, A. O. *Essays on Aristotle's Rhetoric*; Univ of California Press, 1996; Vol. 6.

[xvii] *Business management advice: What Socrates would tell leaders | Fortune*. https://fortune.com/2020/08/25/socrates-business-management-advice-philosophy/ (accessed 2022-12-27).

[xviii] Ehiobuche, C.; Tu, H. DIALOGUE AS A TOOL FOR TEACHING AND LEARNING OF ENTREPRENEURSHIP. **2012**, *19* (1), 11.

[xix] Dennett, P. T. A Socratic Approach to Managing Creativity in Business.

[xx] Dutt, S. *Nietzsche: 5 Secrets To Become Who You Are? (7/8)*. Nietzsche's Philosophy. https://medium.com/nietzsches-philosophy/nietzsches-5-secrets-to-become-who-you-are-e004841f4621 (accessed 2022-12-27).

[xxi] Leiter, B. Nietzsche's Moral and Political Philosophy. In *The Stanford Encyclopedia of Philosophy*; Zalta, E. N., Ed.; Metaphysics Research Lab, Stanford University, 2021.

[xxii] McCallum, J. S. *The Nietzsche School of Management*. Ivey Business Journal. https://iveybusinessjournal.com/the-nietzsche-school-of-management/ (accessed 2022-12-27).

[xxiii] Nicolaides, A. Analyzing Nietzschean Virtue in Business Ethics. *J. Soc. Sci.* **2014**, *41* (2), 187–200. https://doi.org/10.1080/09718923.2014.11893355.

[xxiv] Tajalli, P. A Nietzschean Re-evaluation of Values as a Way of Re-imagining Business Ethics. *Bus. Ethics Eur. Rev.* **2018**, *28*, 1–9. https://doi.org/10.1111/beer.12213.

[xxv] Worden, S. A Genealogy of Business Ethics: A Nietzschean Perspective. *J. Bus. Ethics* 2009, 84 (3), 427–456.

[xxvi] Figueira, T. J.; Brennan, T. C.; Sternberg, R. H. *Wisdom From The Ancients: Enduring Business Lessons From Alexander The Great, Julius Caesar, And The Illustrious Leaders Of Ancient Greece And Rome*; Hachette UK, 2009.

[xxvii] Hedrick, L. *Xenophon's Cyrus the Great: The Arts of Leadership and War*; Truman Talley Books, 2007.

[xxviii] Yenne, B. *Julius Caesar: Lessons in Leadership from the Great Conqueror*; St. Martin's Press, 2012.

[xxix] Caesar, J. *Commentaries on the Gallic War*; Crocker and Brewster, 1865.

[xxx] Barlag, P. *The Leadership Genius of Julius Caesar: Modern Lessons from the Man Who Built an Empire*; Berrett-Koehler Publishers, 2016.

[xxxi] Whiting, K.; Konstantakos, L. *Being Better: Stoicism for a World Worth Living In*; New World Library, 2021.

[xxxii] Sellars, J. *Lessons in Stoicism: What Ancient Philosophers Teach Us about How to Live*; Penguin UK, 2019.

[xxxiii] Coventry, P. Six Ways the Ancient Philosophy of Stoicism Can Help Business Entrepreneurs. **2016**.

[xxxiv] Sherman, N. *Stoic Wisdom: Ancient Lessons for Modern Resilience*; Oxford University Press, 2021.

[xxxv] Stevens, R. *Stoicism for Business: Ancient Stoic Wisdom and Practical Advice for Building Mental Toughness, Productivity Habits and Success in Modern Management!*; Sophie Dalziel, 2019.

[xxxvi] Shaw, B. D. The Divine Economy: Stoicism as Ideology. *Latomus* **1985**, *44* (Fasc. 1), 16–54.

[xxxvii] Swain, T. *Way of The Stoic: Life Lessons From Stoicism to Strengthen Your Character, Build Mental Toughness, Emotional Resilience, Mindset, Self Discipline & Wisdom*; Thomas William, 2022.

[xxxviii] Bowden, H. The Ethics of Management: A Stoic Perspective. *Philos. Manag.* **2012**, *11* (2), 29–48.

Endnotes

[xxxix] Jones, H. B. Marcus Aurelius, the Stoic Ethic, and Adam Smith. *J. Bus. Ethics* **2010**, *95* (1), 89–96.

[xl] Pigliucci, M.; Lopez, G. *Live Like a Stoic: 52 Exercises for Cultivating a Good Life*; Random House, 2019.

[xli] Robertson, D. *How to Think like a Roman Emperor: The Stoic Philosophy of Marcus Aurelius*; St. Martin's Press, 2019.

[xlii] Pandey, J. K. Administrative & Management Principles from Indian Scriptures: A Key of Administrative & Management Dilemmas. *Manag. Today* **2019**, *9* (1), 32–44. https://doi.org/10.11127/gmt.2019.03.05.

[xliii] Mukherjee, S.; Zsolnai, L. Ancient Indian Wisdom for Modern Business. In *Global Perspectives on Indian Spirituality and Management : The Legacy of S.K. Chakraborty*; Mukherjee, S., Zsolnai, L., Eds.; Springer Nature: Singapore, 2022; pp 3–14. https://doi.org/10.1007/978-981-19-1158-3_1.

[xliv] Misra, N. *Better Management & Effective Leadership Through the Indian Scriptures*; Pustak Mahal, 2007.

[xlv] Khanna, U.; Katyal, H. Role of Bhagavad Gita, Mahabharata and Ramayana in Shaping Business Management Practices. *Indian Manag.* **2017**, *1* (1), 75–84.

[xlvi] Srivastava, S. K.; Srivastava, M.; Pandey, A.; Yadav, A. K.; Gupta, A. K. Study of Ramayana and Bhagavad Gita Technical and Managerial Intellects with Enlightening Lessons. *Int. J. Indian Cult. Bus. Manag.* **2022**, *27* (2), 208–226.

[xlvii] Muniapan, B. *The Bhagavad-Gita and Business Ethics: A Leadership Perspective*. Asian Business and Management Practices: Trends and Global Considerations. https://doi.org/10.4018/978-1-4666-6441-8.ch018.

[xlviii] Basu, M. The Essentials of Organizational Management: A Study on the Bhagavad Gita. *Manag. Insight* **2019**, *15* (1), 18–28.

[xlix] Shah, A. K.; Rankin, A. *Jainism and Ethical Finance: A Timeless Business Model*; Taylor & Francis, 2017.

[l] Sanghavi, H. Jainism & Art of Management. *New Vistas Contemp. Manag.* 115.

[li] Inoue, S. *Putting Buddhism to Work: A New Approach to Management and Business*; Kodansha International Limited, 1997.

Endnotes

[lii] Vallabh, P.; Singhal, M. Buddhism and Decision Making at Individual, Group and Organizational Levels. *J. Manag. Dev.* **2014**, *33* (8/9), 763–775.

[liii] Weerasinghe, T. D.; Thisera, T. J. R.; Kumara, R. Buddhism and Organizational Management: A Review. **2014**.

[liv] Lépineux, F.; Rose, J.-J. Spiritual Leadership in Business: Perspectives from Christianity and Hinduism. *Leadersh. Spiritual. Common Good East West Approaches* **2010**, 27–41.

[lv] Alserhan, B. A. *The Principles of Islamic Marketing*; Routledge, 2017.

[lvi] Lewis, M. K. 13. Principles of Islamic Corporate Governance. *Handb. Islam Econ. Life* **2014**, 243.

[lvii] Ibrahim, L.; Adamu, H. B.-Y. Participative Management: A Model of Islamic Perspective of Management (Shura) in an Organization. **2019**.

[lviii] Mohiuddin, M. G. Decision Making Style in Islam: A Study of Superiority of Shura (Participative Management) and Examples from Early Era of Islam. *Decis. Mak.* **2016**, *8* (4).

[lix] Ntshalintshali, M.; Carmichael, T. Applicability of Shaka Zulu's Leadership and Strategies to Business. In *International Conference on Business Strategy and Organizational Behaviour (BizStrategy). Proceedings*; Global Science and Technology Forum, 2011; p 73.

[lx] Allen, C. R. Shaka Zulu's Linkage of Strategy and Tactics: An Early Form of Operational Art? *MA Diss US Army Command Gen. Staff Coll.* **2014**.

[lxi] Smith, A.; Kaminishi, M. Confucian Entrepreneurship: Towards a Genealogy of a Conceptual Tool. *J. Manag. Stud.* **2020**, *57* (1), 25–56.

[lxii] Obschonka, M.; Zhou, M.; Zhou, Y.; Zhang, J.; Silbereisen, R. K. "Confucian" Traits, Entrepreneurial Personality, and Entrepreneurship in China: A Regional Analysis. *Small Bus. Econ.* **2019**, *53* (4), 961–979.

[lxiii] Allen, L. Confucianism and Entrepreneurship in ASEAN Context. In *Entrepreneurship in Technology for ASEAN*; Springer, 2017; pp 161–173.

[lxiv] Xiong, R.; Wei, P. Influence of Confucian Culture on Entrepreneurial Decision Making Using Data from China's Floating Population. *Soc. Behav. Personal. Int. J.* **2020**, *48* (7), 1–12.

[lxv] Zhu, Y. The Role of Qing (Positive Emotions) and Li 1 (Rationality) in Chinese Entrepreneurial Decision Making: A Confucian Ren-Yi Wisdom Perspective. *J. Bus. Ethics* **2015**, *126* (4), 613–630.

[lxvi]Young, J. E.; Corzine, J. B. The Sage Entrepreneur: A Review of Traditional Confucian Practices Applied to Contemporary Entrepreneurship. *J. Enterprising Cult.* **2004**, *12* (01), 79–104.

[lxvii]Romar, E. J. Virtue Is Good Business: Confucianism as a Practical Business Ethic. *J. Bus. Ethics* **2002**, *38* (1/2), 119–131.

[lxviii]Hong, S. B. *The Business Wisdom of Ancient Chinese Entrepreneurs: Timeless Principles for Modern Times*; Partridge Singapore, 2015.

[lxix]Bercu, L. *The 36 Ancient Chinese Strategies for Modern Business*; Lac International Press, 2014.

[lxx]Lafuente, E.; Vaillant, Y.; Vendrell-Herrero, F.; Gomes, E. Bouncing Back from Failure: Entrepreneurial Resilience and the Internationalisation of Subsequent Ventures Created by Serial Entrepreneurs. *Appl. Psychol.* **2019**, *68* (4), 658–694.

ACKNOWLEDGEMENTS

I am deeply grateful for the myriad of support, inspiration, and guidance I received while writing "Ancipreneur: Ancient Paths for Modern Success." This book, would not have been possible without the contributions and encouragement of numerous individuals whose impact on my journey has been immeasurable.

First and foremost, my heartfelt thanks go to my family, whose unwavering support and belief in my vision have been the cornerstone of this endeavour. Their patience, love, and understanding provided me with the strength and peace of mind needed to bring this project to fruition. To my friends, who have been a constant source of encouragement and wisdom, your shared experiences and insights have been invaluable in shaping the perspectives presented in this book.

A special note of gratitude is extended to my professional colleagues and associates, whose diverse viewpoints and expertise have enriched the content of this book. Your willingness to share your knowledge and experiences has been instrumental in ensuring the depth and accuracy of the discussions within these pages.

Acknowledgements

Moreover, I extend my sincere appreciation to Ms Chitra Padmana for invaluable brainstorming sessions that were not only enlightening but also transformative.

In conclusion, I am thankful to each and every person who has walked with me on this path. Your belief in the project and your contributions, both big and small, have been essential to the completion of this book. I am humbled by your support and hope that "Ancipreneur: Ancient Paths for Modern Success" resonates with and inspires every reader, just as your support has inspired me.

Made in the USA
Monee, IL
03 May 2026

49438458R00121